Praise for *China's Generation Y*

Stanat's work is a laudable contribution, as it provides a comprehensive study on China's Generation Y, ranging from its socio-political consequences to the generational gap and the economic factors that ensue. This research builds a more nuanced and objective understanding of this generation.
— **Eva H. Shi,** former editor-in-chief, *Harvard Asia Pacific Review*

As someone who lived and worked in China for several years [as a management consultant with McKinsey & Company in Beijing], I was struck by how closely Michael Stanat's accounts resonated with my own observations and experiences.
— **Christopher J. Fry,** president, Strategic Management Solutions Group

For American companies who want to capitalize on the purchasing power of China's Gen Y, this book is a must-read. The author clearly dispels the myths of Gen Y in China, so Americans beware: China's youth today will propel its nation to be a global economic giant tomorrow.
— **Lee-En Chung,** P.E.

Michael Stanat has probably seen more of the world in his short life than most adults ever will. His combination of facts and impressions of China and its youth make for a quick and fascinating read that will help you prepare for the inevitable upheaval that has already begun.
— **Ira Schloss,** director of corporate planning, Thomas Publishing Co.

Michael Stanat combines a thorough appreciation of the political and economic background to China's Generation Y with a deep personal understanding of this new generation.
— **Joachim E. Seydel**, International Research Consultant, London

Praise for *China's Generation Y*

Michael has captured China Gen Y's zest for technology, entrepreneurship and capitalism. Similar to the teenagers, the Shanghai Stock Exchange and the Internet in China are working out their true value and identity under strict regulations and heavy censorship. The 21st century will provide us with a truly globalized financial industry, in which China's Generation Y will play an important role. Special kudos to Stanat for bringing to light this generation and its future potential in world markets.

— **June Klein**, CEO, Technology & Marketing Ventures, Inc. and author, *Evolution of Trading*

China's Generation Y

Understanding the Future Leaders
of the World's Next Superpower

中國青少年

China's Generation Y

Understanding the Future Leaders
of the World's Next Superpower

Michael Stanat

Homa & Sekey Books
Paramus, New Jersey

FIRST EDITION

Library of Congress Cataloging-in-Publication Data

Stanat, Michael, 1988-
China's Generation Y : understanding the future leaders of the world's next superpower / Michael Stanat—1st ed.
    p. cm.
Includes bibliographical references and index.
ISBN 1-931907-25-0 (hardcover)—ISBN 1-931907-32-3 (pbk.)
1. Teenagers—China—Shanghai. 2. Social surveys—China—Shanghai. I. Title.
HQ799.C552S73 2005
305.235'0951'09051—dc22

                              2005012988

Homa & Sekey Books
3rd Floor, North Tower
Mack-Cali Center III
140 E. Ridgewood Ave.
Paramus, NJ 07652

Tel: 800-870-HOMA, 201-261-8810
Fax: 201-261-8890, 201-384-6055
Email: info@homabooks.com
Website: www.homabooks.com

Edited by Larry Matthews
Printed in U.S.A.
1 3 5 7 9 10 8 6 4 2

This book is dedicated to my brother Scott, my sister Christine, and especially my mother Ruth Stanat, without whom this book would not have been possible.

CONTENTS

Preface   *ix*
Foreword   *xi*
Acknowledgements   *xiii*
Prologue   *xc*

1. Introduction   1
2. Gen Y under Communism   23
3. Lifestyles of a Generation   49
4. Chinese Society and the Individual   87
5. Living Environment   105
6. Dreams and Development   127
7. Gen Y's Inherited Economy   155
8. Purchasing Power and Wants   169
9. A Promising Future   195

Chinese-U.S. Currency Exchange Rates   215
Bibliography   217
Index   219

PREFACE

Christopher J. Fry

Hats off to 17-year-old Michael Stanat for bringing us *China's Generation Y!* His book provides an exciting look into the lives and minds of China's youth, showing us who they are, how they got there, and where they are headed. Stanat brings to life the influences on China's Gen Y—political, cultural, family, economic, and environmental—in such a way that it truly provides a rare glimpse into the minds of today's youth and tomorrow's leaders.

This book is important. China's youth are important. As Mr. Stanat correctly points out, the young, sheltered, impressionable subjects of this book are the leaders of tomorrow's economy. According to the latest Global Competitiveness Report 2004 released by World Economic Forum, China is on track to become the world's second largest economic entity by 2020. And in that year these youths will be 35 years old—a generation of young managers holding together businesses in one of the most important economies in the world.

Stanat helps us to understand who these youths are, what has shaped their development, and what will drive their behavior in the future. As someone who lived and worked in China for several years, I was struck by how closely Michael Stanat's accounts resonated with my own observations and experiences. As a management consultant with McKinsey & Company in Beijing, China, I had the opportunity to interview young job candidates for our entry-level business analyst positions. These candidates were recent college graduates with Bachelor's or Master's degrees from Beijing's top universities – in many ways a sample of China's "young elite." I was amazed at the competitiveness and dedication of these young men and women, at their insatiable desire to succeed, and at their willingness to sacrifice today's comfort for tomorrow's success. Out of several thousand applicants, we hired only a handful of candidates. These young "consultants-in-training" were willing to give 100 percent—of their time, attention, and professional effort—all for the chance to gain some professional experience working for a renowned consulting firm. It was certainly very flattering, and also a sign of the impact that these younger generations are having on the level of competition in the labor force even today.

Will this new generation of future leaders have the skills necessary to steer their businesses, and their country, to continued success? How will these future leaders learn to be leaders if they are sheltered from social interaction by their parents to allow more time for study? Where will Generation Y develop the creativity needed to design and invent tomorrow's products rather than imitate and copy them as is common practice in China today? While no book can predict the future, this treatise provides an in-depth perspective on how Generation Yers are evolving in China and what lies ahead for them in their development.

More than just an insight into this rising generation of Chinese youth and the challenges they will face, this book is a call to action for the Generation Y of the developed world. Unlike many American youths, the Chinese are not sitting around watching TV— they are studying *hard* and struggling to compete for the limited opportunities that mean success in their emerging economy. Stanat shows how the hunger of China's youth, coupled with the expressiveness, creativity, and well-roundedness of youth in the West, creates a new set of standards toward which both groups must strive in order to survive.

Christopher J. Fry is President of Strategic Management Solutions Group, a management consultancy focused on enhancing business performance through analytical decision-making. Mr. Fry lived in China for three years, and was a consultant with McKinsey & Company in Beijing during 2000-02.

FOREWORD

Eva Shi

Globalization and liberalization have freed competitive forces and opened world markets, creating an unparalleled expansion of cultural, political, and economic forces. Such developments have brought about a focus on China—largely due to its size, potential, and recent inauguration into the WTO. Much effort and research have been devoted to the Chinese society and its economic impact, yet there is a scarcity of literature on the core group of individuals who will no doubt play a pivotal role in China's transition—the Generation Y.

China's Generation Y, which some studies describe as a "generation of seekers," is worth examining. These teenagers, born after 1980, are a product of the rigorous one-child policy implemented by the government in the name of population control. Their parents have also endured the extreme regulations of Maoism via the Cultural Revolution and the subsequent mobilization to the countryside (in what was known as *Shang Shan Xia Xiang*). In many respects, they are still indoctrinated with the core philosophies of communism in education, at least to the extent that they wear their red ties while striking a salute to the national anthem. Stories of Chairman Mao and Premier Zhou Enlai are still widespread at the elementary level as a means for children to learn basic grammar while discovering the foundation of their country. Even outside of the classrooms, many of the Gen Yers will have heard war stories of the old days from their parents—a phenomenon I, myself, can attest to.

Yet some might argue that such characteristics linger only on the surface. As Stanat points out, today's China operates under the auspices of "Communism with Chinese characteristics." Many Generation Yers, notably those studied by Stanat, were raised amidst wealth and privilege. There is a remarkable amount of choice available to these youth, ranging from iTunes to luxury handbags. This phenomenon was all the more enforced by the one-child policy, creating a new generation of "little emperors" and "little empresses," as James Watson termed them in *Golden Arches East*. Indeed, the new cohort of individuals embraces consumerism with a vigor that could overwhelm any of the affluent nations.

China's Generation Yers are coming of age during the most consistently expansive economy in the last few decades. They have had a diversity of experiences and aspirations. They can afford to seek better opportunities because of their more positive, optimistic outlook on life, work, and the future. Most of these individuals believe (and rightfully so) that they will be financially better off than their parents. Beyond this, most Generation Yers have also received a healthy dosage of technology immersion. Coupled with the fact that Gen Yers are the most education-minded generation in history (brought up in a culture that highly values education and a workforce that demands it), these individuals are equipped to become an incredibly marketable force to be reckoned with.

While there is a substantial amount of literature on the youth culture of modern Japan (Ted Bestor, Mark Schilling, and Patrick Drazen), there is a dearth of studies done on the youth and pop society of the modern Chinese. This is precisely why Stanat's work is a laudable contribution, as it provides a comprehensive study of China's Generation Y, ranging from its socio-political consequences to the generational gap and the economic factors that ensue. This research provides a more nuanced and objective understanding of this generation. Furthermore, Stanat's work is also accessible to the general public, who may not know much about the historical and political background of China. The central purpose of this book and the further work it hopes to inspire will foster a better understanding of the current conditions of China and its future outlook.

Eva H. Shi holds a master's degree in regional studies East Asia from Harvard University, where she served as editor-in-chief of the *Harvard Asia Pacific Review*. She is currently a consultant for the East Asia and Pacific Poverty Reduction and Economic Management Department at the World Bank.

ACKNOWLEDGEMENTS

I would like to thank SIS International Research (New York) for their funding of the extensive research and their insight into the China youth market based on their years of experience in the global marketplace. Furthermore, I would like to express my gratitude to CBC Research (Shanghai), in particular Managing Director Charles Merkle, who arranged my life as a Chinese teenager and offered his professional staff to assist in the research and appearance of the book. I wish to acknowledge the reviewers of the book: Mr. Chris Fry, Ms. Eva Shi, Mr. Ira Schloss, Mr. Joachim Seydel, and Ms. Lee-En Chung. Special thanks to Ms. Lauren Buckalew, Ms. Maggie Jiang, the Zhengs, Mr. Denton Shen, Ms. Janet Mindes, and Ms. Brenda Lewis.

PROLOGUE

"**C**ome on, children, finish your supper. Imagine those children less fortunate in China who are starving to death. You should be glad that all you have to do is take out the trash. Think about the poor children in China painfully working in sweatshops all day long!"

Statements such as these are often made by American parents to coax children to do the difficult work that children in China supposedly must do on a daily basis. Our society and parents either vocally or implicitly convey these images of a destitute China: one in which poor children guide water buffalos through fields of rice paddies. Aren't these images correct? After all, parents seem to know more than their children. And the majority of American students believe similar ideas about the youth in China. Because the Chinese goods they consume are poor in quality, so must be the people.

These stereotypes, as well as the lack of educational material on the current youth in China, illustrate America's and Europe's profound misunderstanding of the changes occurring in China and what they mean for the youth that experience them.

Western stereotypes of China inculcated in their children are increasingly and rapidly becoming obsolete as China modernizes. China's Generation Y, aged 15 to 24 and approximately 200 million in number, is going to produce the leaders of a country that will have one of the largest economies in the world.

Chinese cities have witnessed unprecedented growth in the past five years. Shanghai's Pudong area went from farms in 1999 to one of the largest economic zones in 2004. Shanghai now boasts the third tallest high-rise in the world and one of the fastest growth rates of any city on the planet. Statistics show that the growth rate in some areas in Shanghai has reached nearly 40 percent. After witnessing countless businesspeople vow that Shanghai would overtake Singapore and Tokyo in the future, I knew Shanghai would be the best place to research a budding youth generation. It seems that Generation Y in China's urban areas has embraced high technology in everyday life with a passion unseen by its fellow generation in America. As China steadily develops itself toward superpower status and embraces the Western "evils" it once sought to quell, Generation Y will increasingly become a major force in China's economic and political life.

Can we ignore Gen Y as we have other young generations for the last fifty years? The answer is no.

Because China's Generation Y is going to be the major competitor for Generation Y's of developed nations, I wanted to overturn Western stereotypes and show how different China's Gen Y is from that of the United States. However, save for the scant, oversimplified newspaper articles on the youth in China, this generation has hardly been described—truly astonishing for such an important group of people. As a result, I planned to take matters into my own hands. I was going to delve into the bustling Chinese world and study today's youth in China, known by marketers as Generation Y, encompassing people born between 1980 and 1989. With the kind help of SIS International in New York City and CBC Market Research in Shanghai, I would add a scientific basis to the project by surveying four focus groups of four segments of the generation. I would complement this aspect of the project with fifteen face-to-face interviews with Chinese youth from various socio-economic backgrounds. The focus group results should be beneficial to people in the U.S.—and the world, for that matter—who are interested in knowing something about Chinese youth, as well as to marketers and business executives who yearn to discover the consumer habits and wishes of this generation. I also planned to live with a Chinese teenager's family in Shanghai for a month. In this way I would be able to reaffirm the responses from the Chinese teenagers and personally experience the way in which China's Generation Y lives.

Throughout the book, readers will discover that Chinese youth are not different from American youth in some ways, but much different in many ways. Similar to the same generation in the United States, Generation Y in China is an up-and-coming group, if not already on the cusp. As a generation, China's Gen Y is acclaimed to be one of the most accepting of consumerism ever since the Chinese government switched its economic priorities from a producer economy to a consumer economy. This change has instilled in China's Gen Y the glamorized values of being relaxed and fulfilled. Experimenting with new feelings of individualism and consumerism, this generation is incredibly receptive to foreign products and will in all probability be one of the first generations in China to openly embrace those of the West.

It is also important to realize that this generation is more than just consumers. China's Gen Y will bring China into a new era of modernization and prosperity. What they do, say, and prefer will not only affect their economy, but also that of the world. This generation will be the one in the future to manage the five "p's"—policies, procedures, products, politicians, and the public—while older generations worry about retirement, financial planning, and new Western "evils" that their country has embraced.

As such, this book provides background information and actual demographic and lifestyle profiles of the country's growing youth population, along with the potential implications for marketers worldwide. On a micro scope, it is my desire to make the voice of China's Generation Y heard by people in the West. On a macro scope, it is my humble wish to help bridge the cultural barriers between East and West.

Chapter 1

Introduction

Welcome to the world of China's Generation Y! This is a world that has until now been relatively uninfluenced by the Western hand, a world where a bustling and burgeoning group of unknown, enthusiastic youth is growing and learning. This world is a place where buildings rise faster than they fall, and where technology spreads faster than in most other countries.

Western thought and bias previously precluded Americans from wanting to learn about this generation. We were taught to ignore China and its vast population, for each person was ostensibly designed as a servant to a hostile communistic state. There persisted an unfounded belief that China could never overtake the West. However, strong indications from its freer market economy, vast population of highly educated employees, and other indications from its new generation of Chinese youth—who are more accepting of foreigners—all point to China's advances on its path to becoming a world superpower.

The Growing Superpower

For most Americans, accepting China as a potential superpower is a tough cookie to chew on, for it ostensibly marks a period of declining American hegemony around the world. Unbeknownst to many Americans, their country has lost most of its competitive industries to foreign countries. It has lost electronics, information technology, manufacturing, aerospace, and, in most cases, luxury goods to countries like Japan and China. The United States is left with car manufacturing, entertainment, pharmaceutical and manufacturing technology, Wal-Mart, and highly inflated real estate. While America loses the industries it championed as its key to superpower status, China rapidly incubates these industries with its vast population of low-paid, educated workers and now more relaxed market-entry laws. Whereas the American middle class is pressed for money as a result of rising expenditures—from the grocery bill all the way to college education—a new middle class in China flourishes, resembling the products of the socio-economic changes in America during the 1950s. While America worried about homosexuals on television and fomented a sanctimonious battle to save the country from liberals, China consistently grew its economy on average by 20 percent for the past twenty years,[1] though some economists find the true rate of growth in 2003 to be around 13 percent.[2] It did so while maintaining a revenue surplus of approximately $500 billion, in contrast to America's trillion upon trillion-dollar deficits that have caused the dollar to plummet, as it will continue to do for several more years. In fact, China's economy was so hot that its central bank needed to slow growth by raising interest rates in order to stop inflation.

China is currently undergoing a renaissance relative to the "dark ages" of the Cultural Revolution in the 1960s. Economy, religion, culture, society, education, and living conditions are all flourishing, causing massive social and political changes in a country that completely rebuked such influences two and one-half decades ago. Likewise, the youth in China during this renaissance are being molded increasingly by the flourishing Western influences that are pervading their country. Ironically, these individuals were born amidst rapid change and confusion, but they are the vehicles that will take China into an optimistic future immersed in technology, consumerism, and economic prosperity it has not seen for centuries.

China's Generation Y accounts for nearly one-sixth of the Chinese population (roughly two-thirds the total population of the United States). Approximately twenty million of these people become adolescents every year.[3]

Yet a large number of Americans still have their heads in the sand. America's long-standing preconception of 1.3 billion people toiling on fields of rice patties neglects the optimistic reality of a growing and extremely motivated capitalistic bourgeoisie in China's urban areas. Others contend that the economic growth will be short-lived, similar to South Korea's lack of momentum in intense development. China, however, differs from South Korea in several significant ways. China has a huge workforce and a massive young population that speak English. China is dedicated to its expansion by allowing gold to be acquired, adjusting interest rates, and adapting its political and economic doctrine by entering in the World Trade Organization (WTO). China has, in the past several decades, made strategic decisions about its development. Unlike Western democracies, China can brutally crush dissent in problematic areas without receiving massive protests from the international community. In effect, the international community has resigned itself to China's administration; shunning China would be an economic nightmare for any nation that makes a clamor about human rights violations.

BusinessWeek claims that China may be headed toward a major economic meltdown because of its financial system's poor investments, which have resulted in many unsuccessful projects and excess capacity. It called for the government to oversee investments and minimize losses of giant state-run banks. The financial system's lack of restraint could potentially slow growth, which could cause major political ramifications in a country that is deciding its own political orientation and future.

However, the power to prevent such a crisis is controlled by the government, which carefully monitors all aspects of life. Educated officials have acted by evaluating select banks' troubled investments. Regulators have slowed foreign investments by 0.5 percent to prevent an overheated economy, and will most likely raise interest rates if a financial crisis is imminent.[4] As long as China prevents its economy from overheating while modernizing quickly enough to curtail unemployment (30 percent of college graduates as of 2004), and prevents rebellion because of the massive divide between the rich and the poor, China can modernize without check. In this manner, it is of little doubt that China will become a massive economic giant, if not a superpower.

China's Growing Economic and Political Might

Even to the skeptic, China's economic might is impressive. China had a Gross Domestic Product (GDP) per capita of $1,000 in 2000; it expects to grow this figure to $3,000 in 2020.[5] Wages of those in professional occupations in large cities are increasing, and companies can currently offer salaries of roughly $7,000 per year. If China plays its cards right by developing at massive speed while maintaining social order and keeping its financial system from investing in poor investment projects that could result in an economic crisis, China's youth in urban regions can expect to earn roughly $800 to $12,000 per year in two to ten years.

With the onset of elevated living conditions and purchasing powers, China's Gen Y will need mortgages to purchase real estate and loans to expand its own companies. In addition, Gen Y will be the first generation to openly invest in the stock market and securities market. Modernization and Westernization will ultimately make Generation Y the major age segment in China with a major potential purchasing power in the future. To some degree, these influences have already distanced the youth from their communistic ties, allowing them to pledge allegiance to Western values of economic prosperity, individualism, consumerism, and, increasingly, a global order. Their access to modern media and products will facilitate their proclivity to purchase items on a global level. As the Chinese economy continues to grow, more foreign firms will participate in a rat race to mold the minds and wants of the easily influenced youth. The improvements in economic and living conditions will make the internal Chinese consumer market one of the largest that will compete with that of the United States.

In addition, China is believed to hold a powerful position in regional politics; indeed, many believe that China is the key to East Asian peace. On a larger scale, China is playing a larger role in macro-politics. It is already one of the five permanent members of the United Nations Security Council, giving it veto power on any powerful Western country's resolution (it has so far vetoed only four times, primarily because of the country-in-question's diplomatic relations with Taiwan).[6] China is growing its army and may receive arms from European countries rushing to end sanctions established after the Tiananmen Square crackdown in 1989.

Politically, China has more power than what meets the eye. The Chinese government has had an important role in the war in Iraq and has propped up the U.S. dollar so the U.S. could borrow even more money. The U.S. is now a major debtor country to a third-world country. If China or Japan, the largest purchasers of American treasury bills, were to stop buying them, the U.S. dollar could collapse.

In this growingly powerful country, China's Gen Y boasts many advantages over its counterparts throughout the world. The Chinese education system turns out some of the best students in the world as a result of rigorous competition that allows only 40 percent of the population to attend the senior high schools that prepare students to take the rigorous entrance exams for university. Not only are the teenagers intelligent, but they are also ambitious to attain their dreams, a motivation sometimes lacking in complacent developed nations. Although China is a third-world country, it is developing at warp speed in some areas and is pumping money into the development of its city centers and infrastructures.

Other Gen Y's vs. China's Gen Y

Gen Y of the United States will remain a strong competitor of China's Gen Y, as its economy is already developed and social order is maintained. America's Gen Y starkly differs from previous American generations because of its dependency on the Internet and television. One marketing company contends that America's Gen Y contrasts with the rebellious Gen X because it is more in touch with its parents and its family's economic decisions. This notion is supported by statistics showing that youth crime, sex, drinking, drugs, suicide, and teen marriage have all fallen since the 1990s, while religion, trust in one's parents, and volunteerism have increased.[7] Although subcultures still flourish, they are not as extreme and subversive as those in the 1980s. In fact, one of the most popular subcultures in American youth is a "preppy" culture that promotes a clean and healthy look.

America's Gen Y will also inherit one of the world's highest GDP per capita and earning power in the world's largest economy. But China's Gen Y has major advantages over that of America, such as low debt, high individual and national savings, textile export advantages, and the largest foreign investment in the world. America's Gen Y bears the weight of troubled social services, the impact of constantly increasing oil prices on its extremely oil-dependent economy as oil reserves dwindle, and the rising political power of the European Union (EU) and China. When America's Gen Y graduates from universities within half a decade, they will find that their counterparts in China will have taken 25 percent of all American Information Technology (IT) jobs.[8]

China's youth must also compete with Europe's Gen Y. The European Union relies on exporting goods overseas in its quest to overtake America as the major economic giant of the world.

Likewise, Europe faces China's cheap exports and a cheap U.S. dollar as major hurdles to its economic goals. The addition of more new countries should make the EU more competitive in exports, but as the living conditions and costs of production rise in Eastern Europe in the near future, the EU will have to export the bulk of its manufacturing outside the block to compete with the U.S. European countries in all probability will struggle with their aging populations coupled with low birth rates and expensive social programs; they are estimated to need 35 million new immigrants to fuel their economies.[9] This may exacerbate racial tensions and further stimulate a growing anti-immigration front.

China's Gen Y must contend neck and neck with its Southeastern neighbor India, which is also rapidly industrializing. Economically, Gen Y's in both countries must vie for outsourcing jobs in Information Technology and human resources. Currently, China is winning the outsourcing battle for manufacturing jobs and flows in capital, and India is winning by its ability to attract Information Technology jobs and flows of skills.[10] India inherently has advantages, such as its advanced technical skills, history of speaking English, and democratic government. India has a very young population: nearly half is under the age of 25.[11] But it faces inhibitors in its economic development, such as caste system discrimination and political parties that will not privatize public companies and take their hands off the economy. The Indian employment market has more drawbacks compared to that of China, as it must deal with affirmative action between castes, while China bases its employment almost entirely on ability and skill.[12] An average Chinese already makes double the salary of an Indian in GDP per capita.[13] Every day China is flooded with more foreign investment, much of which flows from its wealthy neighbors. China has a literacy rate of 91 percent of the population, whereas India's is close to 60 percent.[14] Further, China has leverage among corporations and governments in that it can make corporations lobby politicians to prevent intervention of foreign governments in Chinese matters, and can play a major role in the United Nations, where it has veto power in the Security Council. India, on the other hand, is unlikely to obtain a seat on the Security Council because of its feud with Pakistan.

In other Western countries, Gen Y's future is not as encouraging. In Australia, estimates put the average annual growth rate of per capita GDP over 20 years at 2.25 percent, down from 3.75 percent during the 1990s. The economic future of Australia's Gen Y is compromised by lower birth rate and an expected smaller number of working hours.[15] Japan's economy and culture present a significant problem to Japan's Gen Y, as they deny women's full and equal access in the workforce. Consequently, the working population is nearly halved and, unlike in Western economies, is not augmented by immigrants, potentially resulting in a decreased purchasing power.

Accordingly, Japan's youth will have to increase worker productivity to prevent their nation's GDP per capita from falling in the future; if not, annual GDP rates could drop 1.5 percent annually until 2020.[16] Japanese youth have to work diligently to grow their economy, especially after the Japanese banking crisis in the 1990s, though currently Japanese firms tend to be growing through their investment and marketing in the China market.

In nearly all cases, Gen Y in the future faces burgeoning elderly populations and problems in federal social programs. Unlike China's Gen Y, Gen Y in the developed world faces major drug problems, political hurdles that prevent radical decisions from being made, and problems of complacency.

Yet in spite of the monolithic growth of the Chinese economy and its rising influence everywhere, the world knows very little about China's Generation Y. In contrast, China's teenagers have a better understanding of American youth than American youth have of them. This advantage will help them compete with their American and European counterparts in the future. It is thus of great urgency that the world understands this new Chinese generation, as such knowledge can help formulate economic and political policies in the future.

The Research

Astonished at the lack of information on the issue, I decided to embark on several journeys to China to study this unknown generation. I chose to study China's Generation Y through a combination of resources. The major spine of the project consisted of four focus groups of eight persons each in Shanghai, held in February 2004. These groups ranged from ages 15 to 19, and were divided by gender. For the protection of privacy of the respondents, their full names have been kept confidential. This will protect those informants who gave politically "sensitive" responses. The following is the composition of the focus groups.

The first 30 to 45 minutes of each focus group consisted of a conversation in English between the respondents and me, during which the respondents intimately revealed many details of their lives. Next, each focus group spent an hour and one-half answering questions from a questionnaire in Mandarin conducted by a moderator. The questionnaire consisted of questions about their product preferences and other quantitative data, such as hours worked on homework. The facility was equipped with four translators who simultaneously translated the responses into English.

Accuracy is imperative in relaying the beliefs of a group of people. Likewise, in order to create a research project that was balanced and accurate, I conducted fifteen additional face-to-face interviews with the kind help of CBC Market Research in Shanghai. The questions for the respondents concerned daily life, views on issues, and their perceived differences between American and Chinese teenagers. It was soon clear that this would be the first time for most of the teenagers that someone gave them a voice instead of an order. Ultimately, the formal research aspect of the study involved fifty-five respondents.

Group 1
Consisting of 15- to 17-year-old girls (younger girls)

Last Name	Sex	Age	School	Grade	Monthly Family Income (RMB)	English Ability
Zhou	F	16	The Affiliated School of Jiaotong University	1	3000	Average
Zhang S	F	16	Luwan Senior High School	2	4000	Average
Tao	F	15	Nanhu Middle School	1	5000	Fluent
Zhang Y	F	17	Foreign Language Business Middle School	2	3500	Good
Jiang	F	15	No. 2 Middle School	1	<3000	Good
Xu	F	15	Ganquan Middle School	1	7000	Good
Yao	F	16	Guanlong Senior High School	2	4000	Fluent
Ni	F	17	Fenghua Middle School	2	4000	Good

Group 2
Consisting of 15- to 17-year-old boys (younger boys)

Last Name	Sex	Age	School	Grade	Monthly Family Income (RMB)	English Ability
Cheng	M	17	Technical School of Shanghai Shipyard	2	4000	Good
Zhu	M	17	Jinjiang Hotels Management School	2	<3000	Average
Jiang	M	17	Weiyu Middle School	2	8000	Good
Xu	M	16	Wu'ai Senior Middle School	2	5000	Good
Han	M	17	Commercial Duty School	2	6100	Average
Yang	M	16	Caoyang Middle School	1	9000	Good
Sun	M	17	Yichuan Middle School	2	2000	Good
Qin	M	16	Experimental Middle School of Fudan University	1	3000	Fluent

Group 3
Consisting of 17- to 19-year-old girls (older girls)

Last Name	Sex	Age	School	Grade	Monthly Family Income (RMB)	English Ability
Zhu	F	18	Jianqing Experimental High School	3	5000	Good
Ye	F	18	Nanhu Senior High School	3	4000	Average
Wang J	F	18	Dingxi High School	3	4000	Good
Gao	F	17	Tongbai High School	3	<3000	Good
Wang L	F	18	Commercial School	3	3000	Good
Qiu	F	17	Zhonghua Vocational School	3	4500	Good
Zhang	F	18	Qiyi High School	3	4500	Fluent
Huang	F	17	Shanghai Traveling Vocational	3	5500	Fluent

中國青少年

Group 4
Consisting of 17- to 19-year-old boys (older boys)

Last Name	Sex	Age	School	Grade	Monthly Family Income (RMB)	English Ability
Xu	M	17	Jing Ye High School	3	3500	Good
Wu	M	18	Sun Yat Sen High School	3	6000	Good
Zhan	M	17	Yang Si High School	3	2000	Good
Lu	M	18	Xin Hua Vocational School	3	5000	Good
Wang X	M	17	Yang Jing Middle School	3	4000	Good
Wang J	M	18	Yi Fu Vocational School	3	3000	Average
Xu	M	18	Gang Wan Vocational	3	5000	Average
Yang	M	18	Materials Engineering School	3	4000	Good

中國青少年

The in-depth respondents included the following (last name plus first name initial wherever applicable):

Ying J.	Yu Q.	Jiang Q.	Tao L.	Zhang X.
Li T.	Luo J.	Wen Y.	Zhang F.	Zhu Jip.
Zhu Jil.	Gu Y.	Wang Q.	Ge W.	Xu M.

To put myself in the shoes of China's Generation Y, I decided to experience the daily life of a Chinese youth by living for a month at a home-stay with a local Shanghainese family consisting of a couple and their teenage son. My first-hand observations would be used to complement the information gained from the formal research.

Thus the project became a mix between an anthropological study and market research investigation of China's Gen Y. The intimate descriptions and analysis of Chinese youth's existence are located at the front of the book, and the business opportunity and personal observations are located at the end. The data findings can therefore apply to a wide range of readers, from business executives and adults to teenagers who wish to learn about their future competitors in the global market place.

It is also important to realize that individual Gen Y teens in China are not far apart in their wants and wishes. Communism teaches uniformity in education, political ideology, and interests. Traditional Chinese society also ensures that the ideals of family, life, and education are similar throughout China. As one Chinese proverb states, "The tree that sticks out higher over the forest will definitely be damaged by the wind."

Gu Y., who has traveled abroad and once had an internship in Japan, explains Chinese society:

Do you want to stick out?

It is something about the personality. First I would like to be common with others. Based on that, I will develop my own personality.

Why?

The national education system does not encourage a student to develop his own personality. Our society wants you to be an all-around person; it is not acceptable that you are good at only one thing. Therefore we are unable to do what we really want to do.

You mean you have to consider the social standards or requirements when making decisions?

Yes, we have to be common in many aspects. Based on that, we can have the chance to develop individual things.

The above statements should be analyzed in China's cultural context. Any rudiments of individualism, consumerism, and rebellion should be looked on with significance, as parents of China's Gen Y did not exhibit these characteristics—unlike the baby boomers in the West. In preceding generations, the youth did what they were told to do, meticulously followed tradition, and focused on the welfare of the community instead of that of the individual. Likewise, the combination of new thoughts with traditional views of their parents is indicative of the impact of recently introduced Western values and large-scale changes occurring in the environment surrounding the youth. These modified values have caused a highly palpable generation gap between teenagers and their parents, which is far greater than that in America. The gap has gone so far as to change the ideologies of some teens.

Throughout the book there is a distinction between the urban and rural residents, an important theme in describing the unequal growth in different geographical regions of China that stems from its transition to a consumer economy. The respondents in my case are from the urban population, and some can be classified as being part of the small group of urban middle class, because several of their families earn above 75,000 RMB ($9,069) per year. (At the time there were 8.27 Chinese RMB in one U.S. dollar.) The Chinese Academy of Social Sciences further defines households with assets, including property, ranging from 150,000 RMB to 300,000 RMB ($18,100 to $36,200) as being part of China's middle class. It estimates that 19 percent of the population in 2003 was middle class, and by 2020 the number of people in China's middle class will double.[17]

Why Shanghai?

In an attempt to study the youth that will associate on an equal level with America's Gen Y, I chose Shanghai to conduct the project because of its historical proclivity to Western influences, vast market potential, upgrades in infrastructure, and historic propinquity to capitalism. A city of 20 million residents, Shanghai is one of the wealthiest cities in China. Expectations are for the city's per capita GDP to grow to $7,500 by 2007.[18] Shanghai is also known for its intellectuality and openness to foreign ideas and goods, and the city's experience in modernizing itself will most likely be a model for other cities in China. The number of skyscrapers in Shanghai is remarkable, easily competing with that in any Western city. In fact, the city is leagues ahead of other Chinese cities in modernization and consumerism inasmuch as it will host the 2010 World Expo, thereby further opening up China to the world. Because part of the project is a business assessment of the market, the wealthier and more psychologically and physically developed a region, the easier and more successful a company will be in reaching its consumers.

Another appropriate city for selling consumer products to Generation Y is Beijing. Beijing is smaller in population, but is developing rapidly as a result of winning the bid to host the

2008 Olympic Games. Beijing is China's capital, known for its famous museums, old temples, and palaces. Likewise, the Beijing teenagers are inundated with culture on a daily basis, and are generally very interested in popular culture. At the time of this writing, Beijing teenagers were anxiously awaiting concerts from American musicians such as Linkin' Park, Backstreet Boys, and Britney Spears because most concert tours commence in Beijing. Additionally, teenagers of Beijing are very interested in electronics. On an ordinary Thursday night in Beijing one can expect to see the majority of computers in an Internet café occupied by male and female teenagers answering emails and blasting away monsters in fantasy realms.

However, Beijing is much more politically intense and currently does not boast the pace of modernization and capitalistic values of Shanghai. Gu Y., a Hui ethnic minority who once lived in Hong Kong and traveled to both Shanghai and Beijing, believes the two cities cannot even be compared, instead comparing Shanghai to Hong Kong or New York. Although it is opening China to the world with its hosting of the 2008 Olympic Games, Beijing is home to the largest communist government in the world. Development in infrastructure and human psychology has not proceeded as quickly as it has in Shanghai.

Why Not Hong Kong?

Hong Kong is very developed, but it is being eclipsed by the rapid growth of Shanghai. Hong Kong faces a number of hurdles economically, such as the conflict of integration with Mainland China. Companies now find it hard to compete when prices for property and office space are as high as Hong Kong's skyscrapers. Gu Y. explains other problems:

Do you think that the development level of these cities is about the same?

We still have to wait for some improvement. Because of the weakening of its economy and the financial crisis, Hong Kong's economy is very poor. My aunt has lived in Hong Kong for a long time. The financial crisis really had a large impact; at that time, she almost lost her job. So you could say that Shanghai's ability to repel an economic crisis is stronger than Hong Kong's because it has a better foundation than Hong Kong.

Shanghai is a great market for sports and fashion goods. My home-stay brother and focus group results affirmed that the Shanghainese were more interested in sports than people in Beijing. Shanghai is historically more cosmopolitan and excited about fashion. In fact, Shanghainese women are reputed throughout China to be very fashion conscious and career ambitious. Shanghai has one of the highest proclivities to consumerism of any province in China as a result of its newly acquired wealth from foreign investment and new joint ventures. Along with this reputation, however, remains a negative, prevailing reputation for being excessively concerned about success and money. Many people outside of Shanghai find the Shanghainese to be impolite to outsiders, and therefore do not like Shanghai as a result of these feelings.

My Impressions

As I walked into the facility where I was going to hold the focus groups, I felt somewhat self-conscious. How would they view me? Would they feel intimidated or offended by my questions? Would they be reserved? How far could I push them for information, and at that, how political could I get? What was appropriate to ask teenagers in a communist society? These were the young people who had not been asked for their opinions; in fact, society theoretically made their opinions for them. Thus, wouldn't all respondents have the same opinion? Chinese teenagers often must get their parents' permission to speak to strangers, let alone foreigners. They were taught what their parents wanted them to believe. These questions ultimately played an integral part in my initial conversations with the informants.

I was particularly interested in the reactions of the older groups. Would they feel insulted in talking to a younger American student? Would they give their honest, candid opinions? Would they look down on me as some Americans do on younger people? An automatic disbelief, yet a natural feeling of wanting to trust consumed me before I had even met them. Prior to entering the room with the older respondents, I had to use specific measures such as neglecting to give my age to ensure that they would trust me.

As I led each focus group, I realized that my fears for each group were unfounded. Both groups of girls were very interested in my quest for answers. It was apparent that the respondents aimed to please me and spoke English very well. They were reminiscent of American schoolgirls with their giggly, happy attitude. The older girls appeared to know what they wanted out of life. They were the most gracious for being there and were interested in becoming friends with me and other girls in the group. Although I had been forewarned that the respondents would be nervous, since this method of discussion had been entirely unknown to them, the older females seemed bold, sure of themselves, and the most intelligent.

On the other hand, the younger boys were quite different from the girls in that they were rather reserved. To my dismay, such reservation got the best of them and it was challenging to tempt them even to speak. These younger men seemed uncomfortable about revealing themselves, not sure what their parents would think of their answers. I noticed a difference between American teenagers and Chinese teenagers. Unlike the Chinese teenagers, American teenagers at that age are generally energetic, obstreperous, and unreserved.

Of all the groups, the older males were by far the most relaxed. Frequently there was laughter, and I wondered whether they were laughing at me or whether the joke was an inside one. Unfortunately, I soon ascertained that the translator revealed my age in my introduction to the discussion. This illuminated an important aspect in Chinese culture—the importance of age in relations. Luckily, these respondents were bold and forthcoming with their answers. Most interestingly, their responses indicated that they were tired of being pinned down by their parents, and their demeanor exemplified the overall spirit of China's Generation Y.

In the end, I labeled the younger females as intrigued, the younger boys as shy, the older girls as interested, and the older boys as open. Historically, the Chinese have been known for their xenophobia. However, in conversations with their Generation Y, it was clear that this generation is not xenophobic, as the respondents seemed as interested in me as I was in them.

Perhaps most surprising was the teenagers' resignation to Westernization and lack of opinions in some areas. Their resignation, optimism, and happiness to the prolific, towering office buildings and cranes starkly contrasted with the Western bias of youth in a communist society. Equally surprising, the youth admitted that their generation "blindly" follows trends. This trend-following and their lack of opinions both pointed to the inherent nature of the Chinese education system, familial relations, traditional culture, and the things that Gen Y loves.

The teenagers' appearance was also surprising. I was correct in my hypothesis that the Chinese females would be short and would weigh relatively the same as an American female. For the boys, I originally expected them to be thin and short. However, the majority of the boys were tall and plump, ostensibly the result of overindulgence at the newly arrived KFC and Pizza

Hut. Their appearances ultimately illuminated several other new influences and changes that have gripped this generation.

Unfortunately, it is impossible to show the pictures of the respondents in this book, as the identities of the respondents should be kept confidential, a part of the agreement to entice the teenagers to declare their candid thoughts. Because some respondents gave frank remarks about their personal affections as well as their political ideologies, revealing their identities could spell trouble for those who only sought to aid in the research of the book. However, I am able to explain my observations of the respondents' wardrobes. The females mostly wore clothing in pink, purple, and yellow. One wore a shirt with the "Hello Kitty" logo (Japan), illustrating the pervasiveness of foreign cultural influences. The younger females' clothing looked relatively conservative for their age, considering that a large contingent of their American counterparts commonly wear provocative clothing.

In America, there exists a prevailing stereotype of the Chinese being indigent, wearing torn clothing due to their destitution. What I saw was many urban teens in Shanghai copying the wardrobes of young Japanese. On a Saturday night one would be amazed at the trendy clothing the teenagers wear in popular karaoke clubs.

Their sense of fashion is representative of the pervasiveness of Westernization and the great changes currently occurring within China. More and more teens yearn to be like their Western counterparts, even if they cannot afford to be. In fact, many informants stated that one of their favorite hobbies was window-shopping, as they could not afford pricey clothing. The trends for Chinese youth change more slowly than in other countries. The Chinese youth asserted that fashion changes much faster in the United States, believing that in general, all aspects of life changed faster in America than in China.

Because the purpose of the book is to introduce readers to Generation Y in China, I will commence by clarifying and describing some of the most obvious aspects of life there. Then I will delve into every nook and cranny of the lives of Chinese teenagers. Among the major differences seen by Westerners is a life lived under communism.

Notes

[1]*BusinessWeek,* October 25, 2004.

[2]*The Economist,* May 15, 2004.

[3]http://www.chinabusinessreview.com/public/0407/smith.html

[4]http://news.bbc.co.uk/2/hi/business/3943847.stm

[5]http://www.chinadaily.com.cn/english/doc/2004-04/24/content_326000.html

[6]http://www.auswaertigesamt.de/www/en/aussenpolitik/vn/vereinte_nationen/d_im_sicherheitsrat/vetorecht_html

[7]http://www.brandchannel.com/features_effect.asp?pf_id=156

[8]http://www.internetnews.com/stats/article.php/3331751

[9]http://www.time.com/time/europe/magazine/2000/0703/immigration.html

[10]http://www.atkearney.com/main.taf?p=1,5,1,151

[11]http://www.globalenvision.org/library/7/631/

[12]http://timesofindia.indiatimes.com/articleshow/888078.cms

[13]http://www.economist.com/countries/China/

[14]CIA fact book: http://www.cia.gov/cia/publications/factbook/geos/

[15]http://www.treasury.gov.au/documents/873/HTML/docshell.asp?URL=ai_group.asp

[16]http://www.econ.hit-u.ac.jp/~iwamoto/Docs/Nikkei99.html

[17]http://www.chinadaily.com.cn/english/doc/2004-10/27/content_386060.htm

[18]http://english.people.com.cn/200211/04/eng20021104_106218.shtml

Chapter 2

Gen Y under Communism

As I first arrived in China about five years ago, I braced myself for hours of interrogation I knew would be inevitable. I expected to be patted down at the airport and viewed with a suspicious eye by military men loaded with machine guns. I envisioned men scrutinizing my every move and almost going as far as spying on me during my visit, wondering what my motives were for being in their country. Are these not images of a communist society that are portrayed in Western culture? These perceptions are incorrect—or, at least, less evident.

My easy maneuvering through the airport and experiences in many Chinese cities revealed that communism is "losing ground." The planned economy has been superseded in some areas by a capitalist economy, and the government exerts less influence than it did under Mao. Communism's loss of ground is due to several influences, among them the penetration of the West, economic progress, and the Internet. Further, new consumerist values caused by capitalism emphasize freedom of choice, going against the tenets of the once authoritarian state. It is important to use the term "losing ground" when describing communism today because it may not be faltering as quickly as people in the West would like to believe.

Before some Westerners jump for joy, they must realize that the effects of communism on Chinese youth are still poignant. The parents of these children grew up during the robust years of communism. As a result, they also attempt to heavily instill their beliefs in their sheltered children. For some middle-aged adults, the government is their bread and butter, with millions of employees and absorbing the costs of the government-controlled social services. In addition to being firmly inculcated in the Chinese since the Maoist revolution, communism is complementary to ever-important Chinese values and Confucian thought. Life is structured in a hierarchical system, ranging from clerks in bureaucracies at local and provincial levels to the communist central government—not to mention that the Communist Party of China (CPC) is 66.4 million members strong and still growing.[1] The allure of joining the party among university students stems not from the ideological aspects, but mostly from the relationships the new members can make with other powerful members and the prestige it conveys to employers. The Chinese government also garners some support by taking credit for the economic prosperity and feelings of an optimistic future in China. And although the government is losing power in directing the daily lives of the Chinese people, it still exerts tacit control by using Chinese morals and soft spots to weaken the public's support of anything inharmonious with the government's sovereignty.

The communist education models are based on strict memorization methods advocated by the early philosophers, and deserve credit in spreading the government's thought. In order to graduate from secondary school and university in China (crucial points in the lives of most Chinese), students must take a "politics" class in which they are taught the beliefs and history of communism. Communism—with Chinese characteristics—supports adults' values of their country and government, ensuring that their ideas of education, family, and, to some degree, politics will be instilled in their children.

Media and Surveillance

To maintain its control, the Chinese government still vigorously monitors all types of communication in China. Recently there has been much speculation about the government's attempt to limit access to particular sites on the Internet. The government turns off many sites that it believes will "corrupt" children. Google.com and RadioFreeAsia.org have repeatedly been restricted by the government. Page history and email content are also monitored by the government. The government attempted to curtail the mammoth popularity of the Internet among Gen Y teenagers by simply shutting down some Internet cafés after some parents complained to provincial governments about the Internet's ability to corrupt their children.[2] In addition, the government has a strict code of law to which Internet cafés must adhere, including one stipulation that prohibits their location within a 200-meter radius of a school. However, the ever-increasing availability of the Internet and the number of Internet users (80 million as of 2004)[3] are making it increasingly difficult for the Chinese government to control information access to "immoral" material, such as violent material. The government has become even stricter after a fire burnt down an Internet café killing 25 people; in just a three-month period the government closed down 12,575 such cafés.[4] The government has correctly assessed the importance of these precautions, as China's Generation Y has a tendency to be swayed by influences and information. The memories of June 4, 1989, in Tiananmen Square in Beijing are still too vexing for communist leaders.

The government also actively takes measures to monitor telephone communication. China is now the largest mobile phone market, with nearly 300 million users at the end of 2004,[5] and is steadily and rapidly growing year by year. To mitigate dissidence, the government monitors phone conversations and text messages (a popular communication medium for Gen Y) at 2,800 monitoring centers.[6] If one hears a muffled delay during a phone conversation, the government is most likely listening to the call. Foreign travelers have been thrown out of the country for comments the central government thought seditious. Beijing monitored the phone conversations of millions during the SARS epidemic in 2002, and ultimately ordered the arrests of about a dozen people for their purportedly seditious messages.

Although the majority of Chinese youth have remained loyal to their country's communist roots, some are beginning to reject some aspects of their society. China's youth are becoming more and more dissimilar from previous Chinese generations. They are beginning to date, a practice that their parents would have never considered until matriculation into university. They are beginning to yearn for the material items once branded by their beloved leaders as "Western Evils." They are spending more of their free time on the Internet instead of ruminating and working on the welfare of the state. Many teenagers identified governmental corruption as a significant problem in China. One teenager even stated that he wanted to change the government into one like that of the United States. Along with the government, he wanted to reform Chinese society and its education system.

However, it cannot be said that the youth are rebelling against the government's politics more than against traditional culture. After the discussions I was convinced that Generation Y in China knew very little about politics, less than its preceding generation and perhaps less than American teenagers. China's Generation Y, unlike its parent generation, is not being massed like the Red Guards in the streets of Beijing during the Cultural Revolution (1966-1976), advocating the abolishment of property for the benefit of the proletariat. On the contrary, China's Gen Y is mostly concerned with school, relaxing, buying new products, and socializing with friends.

The Current Situation

Several teenagers contended that there are growing gaps between the "haves" and "have-nots" in China. Their thoughts are not unfounded: since the early 1990s, there has been a growing polarization of the society as a whole. Estimates of the number of poor citizens rose by nearly a million people, and last year marked the first increase in the number of those earning $75 or less since the economic reforms of the 1980s.[7] The National Bureau of Statistics of China shows that the average urban per-capita income is nearly three times the income of rural residents. When one teenager revealed his thoughts on this problem, he replied that the gap would widen even further, but would eventually improve in the distant future.

The government often exacerbates the problem by taking land from the rural peasants to build institutions for modernization, such as highways and factories.[8] It is also believed to favor urban dwellers by separating the peasants from the urban dwellers to prevent an uprising, essentially precluding the peasants from the benefits of socialism and the right to live in prosperous cities. In many cases, schooling in rural areas is untenable, as the costs of tuition are several times more than the average yearly income of farmers. At the same time, drug usage and egregious corruption have significantly increased in recent years.[9] The government is following Deng Xiaoping's famous statement, "Let some people get rich first," maintaining that when more people get wealthy, they will share their wealth with the rest of society.[10]

Generation Y finds corruption in the Communist Party of China (CPC) as one of the greatest problems facing the nation. The large, opulent houses and luxurious German vehicles of party leaders make the youth question the government's mishandling of the ideals of Mao Zedong. Corruption has become so rampant that the central government has launched a campaign against it. In the last several years, 1,252 officials suspected of corruption have committed suicide, and 8,371 officials fled the country.[11] It is often enticing for officials to take bribes because less powerful officials of varying statuses and duties are paid relatively the same amount in adherence with socialist doctrine. Furthermore, the children of party officials are often the most corrupt. These privileged offspring have power and connections that make them far superior to the average citizen. This troubling trend has assuredly alienated the older members of Generation Y and young adults.

Another attitudinal change in the youth toward government stems from the country's ideologies and responses to revolts of the past. Many teenagers have accepted some of the ideologies long associated with communism, but discredit others. It was evident during my interviews that China's youth are slowly forming their own opinions. Most rebuke the teaching styles of their martinet teachers, view their lives differently from their parents, and have bigger dreams than do their parents. Some simply do not want to be trapped by their parents' plans for their future and the overbearing rules that restrict them.

Many males stated that they just want to live their life happily and of their own will. "I do not want to be restrained by anyone," says one older male. This statement and those of many others who have expressed similar ideas clearly show that this constrained Gen Y is tired of being ordered around by figures of authority who always tell him how to live.

Increased influence of the media has illuminated the differences between Chinese and Western youth and has increasingly become a silently growing tumor for Chinese society and government. Amazingly, one teen used an example from television to show the difference between an American parent and a Chinese parent when their children climbed a tree in their sight. When she saw her child in his ascent, the American mother clapped her hands and cheered her child to reach a higher branch. In contrast, the Chinese mother screamed and yelled at her son to get down from the tree.

Another phenomenon to affect the attitudinal and cultural makeup of influential youths throughout China is the growing ranks of federations and associations that are helping to shape and mold the young minds of Chinese citizens. One such entity is the Beijing-based All-China Youth Federation (ACYF), which provides many programs for Chinese students to study and learn abroad by establishing exchange programs with 250 organizations in more than 130 countries. The ACYF has also launched activities in sports, games, culture, and scientific and technical fields, such as the "Tour de China" cycling event.

The China Youth and Children Research Center (CYCRC) of Beijing is an institution that seeks to help the Chinese youth succeed in life, as well as in work. The group, though more of a think tank than a participatory program, funds research and educational programs that focus on the proper cultivation of youths and addresses modern problems that Gen Y must face.

Ultimately, these organizations, often working in tandem with the central government, attempt to cultivate the youth during China's transitive process from a communistic state to a freer government.

Impact of China's One-Child Policy

One of the influences forming the attitudes and personalities of Generation Y is China's infamous one-child policy. All of the respondents were from the urban areas and grew up under this policy—that is, without siblings in the nuclear family. Nearly 80 percent of all urban children who attend primary school and day care programs are the only child in their family.[12] It is important to take notice of this policy and its implications for Gen Y because it greatly affects the way Chinese youth view their life, society, and the world around them.

In China, a child's life dramatically changed with the one-child policy that began in 1979 as a result of a sweltering population. The central government realized that Mao Zedong's encouragement of Chinese women to have as many children as possible to overtake the West was not as perfect as it appeared to be twenty years later, when resources rapidly dwindled. Although globally controversial, the policy has helped control the population by reducing it by 250 million, although China still carries one-fifth of the world's population.[13]

Much criticism has resulted from this one-child policy because of the tendency to discriminate against females, leading to abandonment, abortions, adoptions, or the hiding of female children. Because purchasing power has improved for much of the population, pregnant women are more able than ever to identify a female fetus by ultrasound, allegedly increasing abortion rates over the years.[14] Some critics claim that this policy has increased the murdering of female infants, because many parents purportedly have killed their first-born female in order to try again for a male. Critics also contend that more Chinese women commit suicide during childbirth age as a result of ignominy and excessive pressure to produce the desired child. Many families give their daughters up for adoption in order to try again for a male child. One mother, Pan Juan, who gave her daughter up for adoption, replied in the *Washington Post*: "Many people do that. They just bundle the child up and leave it with the government. Perhaps she made it to America."[15]

As a result, the government leads a campaign to promote contraceptive and abortion services in order to control the harrowing issues that arose. Later marriages, smaller families, and longer intervals between births were encouraged. To further discourage Chinese couples from having more than one child, government-granted incentives, such as housing, schooling, and health services, were given to those who followed the one-child policy. In the nation's largest cities, such as Shanghai and Beijing, severe penalties still abound for those who break the one-child policy, such as loss of job, public admonishment, and large fines. Strategically, the one-child policy allows the government to assert its control over the birth and development of the child, thus increasing its power.[16]

In many parts of China today the policy is ignored because more people with greater incomes claim that it is worth having more children if they can pay the fine, especially those in rural areas who need help farming the land and with other chores. Wan Baoqi, a mother of three living in the village of Dalu, stated in the *Washington Post*: "The real reason [for needing boys] is that we need someone to fetch water, to guard our orchard, to work in the fields, and to care for us when we get old." Economic growth and other transformations are creating loopholes in the system.

The one-child policy has thus affected the interpersonal relations among family members. Parents who abide by the one-child policy adorn their single child with much affection and economic resources because that child is the sole perpetuator of the family line and the only way for parents to realize their own unfulfilled dreams.

Imagine having a whole generation without siblings in the nuclear family. Those teenagers would have everything they want; they would enjoy the full attention, resources, and help of their parents. Thus Gen Y singletons are unaccustomed to giving up attention around other people. The teenagers may not see a need for siblings when they have cousins, whom they treat as brothers and sisters and denote as such. Gen Y teenagers in China have adapted to their one-child society and, in all probability, could not imagine life with siblings.

The babying, as it were, appears to be a major negative for this generation because Chinese youth rely so heavily on their parents for guidance. It is obvious to an American that Chinese youth are dependent on their parents and seem immature compared to American youth. Chinese youth tend to be significantly overprotected by their parents yet spoiled in the process, generally receiving better health care, education, and, of course, brand-name toys and clothes. The translated words in Chinese for these spoiled, single children are *xiao huangdi* or "Little Emperor," because they are so spoiled. Though parents are the ones who are overprotective and accommodate their children's every need, they are often the ones who view their children as spoiled, selfish, and lazy.

Relations with Their Parents

In spite of their parents' babying and close relations, nearly all of the teens in the study believe that there is a significant generation gap between them and their parents. Some used adjectives such as "old-fashioned" and "overbearing" to describe their parents. The extent of the generation gap is illustrated with countless statements and hints:

Zhang X.: "…Like when I do homework, I like to be by myself, and I don't want people next to me interfering. When I am practicing, I come home a bit late, you know? Normally everyone else has already eaten dinner, and then I sit by myself and eat, and on one side is my mom and on the other my grandma. They watch me eat, and I can't stand it. I just don't like the feeling that I am being supervised by others."

Responses from the older male focus group:

What would make you happy?

Wang: It'd be great if nobody supervised me. Then I could do whatever I want.

Lu: I like doing whatever I want.

Zhan: I need my own space.

Wu: I do whatever I like.

Xu: So do I.

So, some topics you can talk to your parents about and some topics you can't. Then what can you talk to them about?

Yang: My cell phone fee.

Older females who generally are closer to their families found many differences between them and their parents.

What is the difference between you and your parents?

Zhang P.: We are much more fashionable. More open.

Wang L.: Thinking.

Huang: We and our parents have different values.

Zhu: Very traditional.

Females usually hold secrets of love to themselves because their parents are generally more overprotective of females, and because the parents would associate that feeling with an indication of youth dating, a major taboo for the old-fashioned parents.

Chinese youth are taught to honor and obey their parents like any child, but are left with little room for individuality. Ideas, wants, and needs seem to be instilled in the brains of Chinese youth by their parents. However, their ideas and hopes of individuality sharply contrast with those of their parents. Despite their parents' high hopes for them, it was astonishing to discover how the youth did not really know what they wanted to be when they grow up, especially those on the cusp of graduation. And a large number of informants who had an idea about their future complained that their ideas were in sharp contrast with those of their parents.

Education in China

If you compare Chinese young people and American young people, do you think there is a difference?

Americans definitely don't read as much as Chinese people.

You think their reading ability is not as good as the Chinese?

Yes. But they definitely care about individuality; that's the difference between the two countries, the difference between Chinese and Western cultures.

You think they are a group with very strong individualities?

Yes.

Now which of these do you think is better?

I can't say this is good and that is bad. What's good is that Chinese people have a very broad knowledge of things. In the future, when they study anything, they will be able to grasp it very quickly. That is an advantage. Foreigners, if you ask them about science, they only know about one little part; and if you ask about something else they will not know. Chinese knowledge of science is not the same. They have a very broad knowledge, and will have knowledge about their own specialties as well as those of others.

It's more complete?

Yes. In this and in other areas there are pluses and minuses. If you study a lot, maybe it will have an effect…but if you study just a few things, what will happen if you need to know something else?

— Gu Y.

Education is very significant to Gen Y, ranked as the most or second-most important aspect of their lives. The education system molds the way Chinese youth think, and understanding the Chinese education system can help us understand the ideas and viewpoints of people like Gen Y.

A common perception of the average American public school held by American teens is an institution of folly, incorporating educational study with intense peer pressure and socialization. The academic curricula in many schools are rather difficult for many students, and cheating in many schools is rampant. After the school day is finished, the student faces peer pressure that might affect his or her behavior. Those students who wish to obtain high grades are often ostracized by fellow classmates for being "nerds." Many students speak out irresponsibly and find themselves in trouble with the school's administration. Students divide themselves into a rigid social caste system composed of jocks, cheerleaders, computer nerds, gangsters, and drama fans. Consequently, many students expend excessive amounts of energy away from schoolwork in order to fit into a clique.

The school environment in China is far different from that in the U.S. The Chinese are not nearly as self-conscious and peer-pressured as most Americans. When the teens in my study were asked if they were subjected to peer pressure, the majority shook their heads and appeared confused, as if to wonder why anyone would ask such nonsense. They indicated that bad adolescent behavior, such as drug usage and binge drinking at parties, is generally frowned on by Chinese teenagers. Many teenagers in China believe that binge drinking and other poor behavior are part of the "bar culture" in the West that could disrupt their grades. Drug usage is not as high in China, as possession can result in seven years in prison. It is very typical of American teenagers to listen to music, but not to sing it in front of their friends or any type of crowd because of intense peer pressure. In China, teenagers express themselves without a strict social code and are somewhat oblivious to what others think. They even sing karaoke without being inebriated!

Esthetically, the American and Chinese school systems are quite different. Unlike in America, every student attending school in China must wear a uniform, with a few exceptions in rural areas. Students who forget their uniform unique to their school would not be able to attend class and would have to confront their strict teachers. During my home stay, the son of the family showed me his school uniform, which, in spring and autumn, consisted of white pants and shirt with blue stripes (similar to an Adidas jump suit). The uniform also changes with seasons. In the summer, students wear short-sleeved uniform shirts and shorts in the same style. The winter uniform usually consists of long pants, a long-sleeved shirt, and a pullover in cold regions.

Tuition for students in high school is paid mostly by parents and not, surprisingly, by the government. All teenagers mentioned that their parents pay anywhere from 1,000 RMB ($125) to 5,000 RMB ($600) per year, depending on which school they attend. Those who attend the more prestigious schools often pay more. The expensive tuition and its frequent increases are a great incentive to make teenagers study harder. Some families are so dedicated to getting their children into college that they make it their sole reason for working. Yet the steepness of tuition often makes it nearly impossible for those from low-income households to ever receive a higher education, and often precludes many parents from purchasing some consumer goods.

If a student's parents can afford for their child not to work, they will in all probability not insist on it, as earning good grades is extremely important, or even imperative, to obtaining a "good job" after graduation from college. This trend is popular in the wealthier urban areas of China, where students live considerably better than their compatriots in the west and south. It is the ultimate goal of the parents and the Chinese society to get their children into college. The students understand that school and homework are their prime duties and their *raison d'etre* during adolescence.

In China, the schools are much more exacting than many schools in the West. In contrast to American culture, Chinese culture does not have a taboo against one's life being completely consumed with school, most likely due to China's economic status as a developing nation. A college education in China is not open to everybody, and finding a well-paying job is far from facile.

At the age of six, Chinese children begin to attend a primary or elementary school for six years. The students learn Chinese, mathematics, music, and physical education. They later learn English, chemistry, physics, and biology. The students then obtain a graduation certificate and move on to junior middle school at age twelve. There the students learn Chinese, math, physics, chemistry, politics, history, hygiene, physiology, and English, etc., for three years. Before graduation from junior middle school at the age of fifteen, all middle school students take a high school entrance exam that decides whether they will go to a college prep senior high school—which ultimately prepares them for entering university three years later—or a technical, or vocational school, where they learn subjects such as cooking, nursing, and engineering for joining the workforce in two to three years.

The competition for the high school exam taken during the summer is so rigorous that only half of the total number of junior middle school graduates in China pass it each year, forcing much of the other half, largely those in rural areas, to work to make a living.[17] High scorers who end up at college prep high schools, the most prestigious high schools, account for only a quarter of the total number of junior middle school graduates in the nation. They study sciences and humanities at these college prep high schools to prepare for the National College Entrance Exam that faces them at the age of 18. Out of these lucky college prep school students, only half pass the exam and can go on to college, roughly 13 percent of the total number of people at that age.[18] Those who pass the National Exam will mostly enroll at universities in the departments the students specified on the day of their exams. High achievers who have high enough scores to go on to the best universities in the country, such as Peking University in Beijing and Fudan University in Shanghai, have the possibility of doubling their income.[19]

So what about those technical or vocational school students who do not have a chance to get into a university? They generally accept their fate of earning less. One older male attending vocational school replied:

What satisfies you?

I will try my best to work hard for 10 or 20 years. It's better to have some unexpected wealth. After 10 or 20 years, I will

37

play mahjong at home and there will be some kids around me. It's like that.

Do you want a peaceful life?

Yes. After 10 or 20 years, I will be over 40. What else can I do? You won't have any breakthroughs in your career. If you want to have a career development, you must plan it in advance.

Lauren Buckalew, an analyst at CBC Research Shanghai who has gone to school in both the U.S. and China, explains, "In China's not-so-distant past in the late 1970s and 80s, a good education led to a coveted 'good' job—'good' meaning able to guarantee one lived above the poverty line. Parents who grew up during China's economic opening after 1976 are especially sensitive to education's role, and in turn a top university's role, in securing a good job and high salary. In choosing a career, a child's personal interests or skills are less significant factors than a job's prestige, wage level, and the parents' wishes for their child. As such, by high school, students are focusing entirely on the immediate future—the college entrance exam. After that, little is left for them to consider. Parents and teachers will help them choose a lucrative major, and they will find a lucrative job."

Buckalew continues, "Chinese students bear much pressure from parents and teachers to excel at test-taking, or, to be more exact, to excel on one test in particular, the College Entrance Exam, which is pass-fail and offered only once a year. It is the single most important test in a Chinese student's life, and is the object around which studies from kindergarten until 12th grade [grade 3]—a year dedicated entirely to review for the exam— revolve. This one exam is so important because it alone decides if a child can attend a university, and if that university is average or superior. Graduates of a superior university are guaranteed good, stable, prestigious jobs their whole lives."

Today's incredibly difficult college entrance exam is similar to the Confucian bureaucratic examinations used in past dynasties, as it poses specific questions regarding minute facts that provide a strong foundation for further knowledge, such as naming the general who won the such-and-such-war against the so-and-so dynasty. Accordingly, at school students learn by memorizing articles and dates. My home-stay brother was astonished when I revealed that most American teachers do not force students to memorize entire articles in foreign languages in a single night. He declared that if he missed a word in reciting an English poem, he would be yelled at and humiliated in front of the class.

Chinese teaching methods also preclude students from asking questions. Asking a question would indicate that the flawless teacher had made a mistake, thus insulting the teacher. If students have a question, they must ascertain the answer by themselves at home or through fellow classmates. Essentially, in the Chinese school system the teacher is the drill sergeant and the students are the soldiers. The entire setup of the Chinese school system is imperative to a communist government because the strict memorization of Chinese philosophies and history builds crucial self-identity and nationalistic thoughts; moreover, it teaches a citizen to obey without asking any questions. Thus the sky is blue because that is the way it is. The lack of creativity is partially an impetus for the youth's ready acceptance of trends and fads. The youth's creativity is most often stifled as students search for models instead of inventive solutions to problems.

Xu L., female, 15: …I like cartoons very much.
Will you draw a picture for us later on?
Xu L.: I am not good at painting, but good at imitating.

A large number of Chinese students find this method ineffective. As one female states, "They feel like they are filled with knowledge, and we are forced to learn this and that. It's like feeding a duck." American education methods, in one teen's eyes, "focus on the improvement of the capabilities of the person."

After numerous pleas from students and experts, the Chinese Ministry of Education has agreed that the traditional learning methods stymied real-world learning and instituted new elective classes for students in ten provinces.[20] The new classes specifically incorporate discussion-style teaching methods that encourage critical thinking. It has also tried to integrate sexual education in its curriculum to be in line with modernization, but many teenagers and experts find the program inadequate. One study finds that barely 15 percent of Shanghai and Jiangsu (a province close to Shanghai) teenagers had learned about sex from their parents or teachers.[21] Traditional Chinese customs are preventing the first published sex education textbook from being distributed amongst teenagers. For many parts of China, sex education courses first became available only in 2003, primarily because of parents who did not want their children to learn about topics that in their eyes were inappropriate and could interfere with school.[22] As of today, the sex education curriculum for many schools consists of a brief introduction to human anatomy and strict warnings from teachers to abstain from intercourse.

The number of Chinese youths who have enrolled in educational exchange programs to the United States, Europe, and elsewhere has grown dramatically. After their studies, many have returned to China and passed on their insight to China's leading universities and technical schools. Moreover, many have taken the skills learned at Western universities to China and created their own companies, taking advantage of cheap labor and making large profits.

Pressure, Pressure, Pressure

An extreme example of the impact of the pressures caused by school and the essentiality of education is illustrated by the story of Zheng Qingming. The son of a peasant couple, Zheng was

40

eighteen years old living in Pujia, an impoverished region in Sichuan province. Although Zheng was purportedly excelling in his academics, he could not afford to pay the eighty dollars in order to take the university entrance exams. His family stated that they had fallen upon difficult times as the mother became sick and the father lost his job. Zheng's teacher embarrassed him in front of his class to pressure him to pay the fees. Several hours later, feeling that he had no future and that his honor was tarnished, Zheng stepped out before an approaching train.

Because the education system is so competitive as a result of the mammoth high school population (76 million adolescents aged 15 to 18 in 2004)[23], the students face immense pressure to succeed from their schools, peers, and parents. Unlike in the United States, the Chinese schools force children to study by humiliating nonperformers in front of their peers, compelling most students to do what they are told. Teachers readily dole out pressure because their performance is rated and their wages determined by the high school entrance exam and university entrance exam as well. For instance, Jiang, a 15-year-old female, complained, "My teacher said, 'Since you decided to come study here [secondary high school], you must do your best to do well in the university entrance examination!'" Parents also put on stress. When one mother signs her child up for extra classes to get ahead, all other parents will follow.

If the students do not do what they are told, they will not be considered "cool" by their peers as they are in America. Students may even be ostracized by individuals who obtain satisfactory grades, as parents will often lend their important approval to friends based on their academic grades. One female mentioned that her mother disapproves of her female friends interested in fashion because in her eyes fashion sense specifically takes away from studying. If students still do not obtain satisfactory grades and are not convinced by humiliation and peer opinions, many teenagers have indicated that their parents will beat them until they receive better scores. The competition has become even fiercer as China morphs its economy into a market economy, which heightens earnings but lowers job security. Ultimately, these measures function to make both Chinese students and school environments among the most competitive in the world.

But there are drawbacks to the Chinese school system. The immense quantity of first-class students forces all students to endure a great degree of pressure. The significance of the entrance exams is inculcated on the minds of students as soon as they begin school. Because prospects for the future of many students are determined by one exam, the pressures of authoritarian teachers and the stress from unrelenting parents make school the most difficult, yet most important, aspect of their life.

Pressure is transmitted through daily contact with parents:

Do you give your family members presents on their birthday?
I gave my mother a bunch of flowers. As for my dad, his biggest wish is that I can enter a famous university. He doesn't care about anything else.

— Gu Y.

Accordingly, school was ranked high by most of the teens; one female ranked school higher than she did her parents. All but five other informants in the study believe that school is either the most or second-most important aspect of their lives. It is often difficult for students to balance out their stress because of their parents' sheltering and a palpable generation gap that makes communication difficult. As a result, many Gen Yers look toward the Internet and some Western media to fill such a communication void.

The tremendous pressures of the school and other pressures that go along with the Chinese school system take away the personalities of many students. Before speaking to the youth, I hypothesized that Chinese teenagers would have only a slightly smaller vocabulary of political beliefs than did the youth in the 1980s, but I was completely wrong. It turned out that the teenagers do not know much about politics or themselves at all. Most are relatively immature and undeveloped vis-à-vis Western students. Most had no ideas on what they wanted to do after graduating from a university. Regrettably, the only truly solid dream most individuals had was of a high-paying occupation. Parents exacerbate the situation by shielding any possible obstacle and outside-of-school influence away from their children, reasoning that any potential deviation will have an effect on the teenagers' grades. Many Chinese youth do not have their own opinions or personalities. For example, one student outside of the study posted on her Internet blog (bulletin board) that even though she had graduated from university, she had no opinion on the death penalty. Such is the case with all the teens in the study: most of them had never been asked their opinions the way I was; moreover, many had not given their opinions before. It looks like Chinese teenagers are only sure of schoolwork and family. Curricular reforms will help, but the influences of the Internet and television will only work to further shelter China's Gen Y.

The older boys are not easily resigned to the assigned amount of work. Some of the boys are so turned off by school that they rush home to play video games that take them away from stress and allow them to relax. But when these male teens were asked what they wanted to do in life, many did not know. Several teenagers on the brink of graduation stated that they wanted to start a business but had little idea what they wanted to start. Others had even vaguer ideas of their future. One of the few solid ideas expressed of their future was of earning loads of money and relaxing. Their apathy is partially caused by the incessant stress of school and parents and the difficulty in managing their problems. Certainly, all this generation is not wasted. Many females want to be doctors, lawyers, and businesswomen; a few showed an interest in helping society by reforming the Chinese education system and government.

China's school system, which champions uniformity, thinking inside the box, and a hierarchical authority, inherently poses problems in planning and management. This is the case in city planning and logistics in Shanghai. Recently the Shanghai government commissioned a massive high-speed train called the Maglev connecting the international airport in Pudong to the center of Shanghai. The magnetic levitation train is an impressive technological marvel for China. However, planning for the train is flawed, for the train leaves from the airport and goes to nowhere. In fact, to even take the train from the airport one has to take the train to a remote train station located in the middle of nowhere, and then take a long taxi ride to the center of Shanghai. China also lacks efficient logistics in trade and manufacturing. Chinese firms often rely on Western logistics firms to plan for the transportation of goods. The lack of modern logistics can be attributed to the teaching methods and skills taught at China's schools. Students are taught to memorize models and decisions that are not commensurate with those of the competitive, modern marketplace.

Gen Y's Homework

After school, most of the teens cannot just go out to play and have fun; they must go home and finish their homework. The amount of homework usually increases in the second to third year of high school. Some students in intense school programs attend half days of school on Saturday and use the weekends for tutoring and finishing an even larger-than-normal homework load. Specifically on homework, half of the young females (half in high school and half in middle school) spend more than six hours outside of the eight-hour-plus school day doing their homework, while the other half work three to four hours. On average, the younger boys in middle school spend from one to two hours each night on homework, while the older boys spend even less time and rate homework of low importance as they near graduation. Males unanimously agreed that the girls are more serious and are more thorough, and realized that their female counterparts may overtake them in future school years.

Some of the older boys' lack of interest in college defies statistics, which boast a 91 percent literacy rate for those older than 15. Expanding literacy rate has helped the academic ranks of those students who are attending colleges in China. This helps Chinese youth today excel as they never have before. Educational institutions are attempting to expand their capacity to make way for more students, but at the expense of increasing student competition.

Among the most popular extracurricular activities for the teenagers in my study are badminton, swimming, basketball, tennis, and soccer. However, universities exert far less influence on participation in extracurricular activities than on making the grade. Because high schools solely emphasize the grade, students have little time to engage in new activities and interests. This places average Chinese students at a disadvantage when they apply to American colleges that look at the quality of student achievements outside of school almost as much as they do those inside of school. Ultimately, these communal extracurricular activities are being superseded by individual activities centering around the Internet.

Social Issues

Suicide in China is not at all uncommon for Chinese youth. In fact, 19 percent of all deaths of people aged 15 to 34 are caused by suicide, and 42 percent of the world's suicides occur in China.[24] Chinese culture's lack of taboo against suicide is most likely a cause for its prevalence.

Another issue frequently mentioned as irritating by teenagers is the school system's influence on their personal lives. The most significant influence is the school's responsibility to punish teenage daters. The school enforces a rule against an important social faux pas—dating during high school. Parents are content with this policy, as they believe dating will cause the student to slide into poor grades. Schools have been known to punish perpetrators, with the first offense for dating generally being a lecture from the teacher. The next time a teacher suspects that a couple is dating, he/she will call the parents of both students to the school and demand that the parents end the relationship. Unlike in America, Chinese parents do not defend their children against school punishments.

The rules against dating have become more lenient, since dating is not as taboo as it was in the adolescent years of Gen Y's parents, a sign of Western influence. In fact, many teenagers in the study candidly admitted that they, or their friends, date. Two male teenagers shocked the older moderator when they mentioned they had girlfriends and that their parents did not care. The teens also believed that parents are generally more protective of females than of males. Although the parents accept their sons' relationship, they still believe that their grades will fall and that dating should wait until university.

Indeed, it can be seen that China's Generation Y is becoming more American because Chinese teenagers sue their schools for invasion of privacy. In 2004, students at Fuxing High School in Shanghai were shown security camera footage of a couple kissing and other disruptive behavior. Teachers tried to obstruct the identities, but students found out and harassed the lovers. Though the couple sued the school for 5,000 RMB and sought an apology from the school administration, they lost the case.[25] The incident, however, has left its mark on Chinese society: the kiss caused much controversy that has resulted in numerous articles in newspapers and a published book by the male party at issue. The situation not only shows the new phenomenon of

46

dating in Chinese schools, but also the problems of and objections to public surveillance, currently regulated by amorphous, unwritten legal boundaries.

However, not all teenagers are completely disobeying their parents' decree and submitting to Western culture, for several of the younger teens in my study believe that they are too young to date.

Lasting Impressions

I cannot resist offering my lasting impressions of China's Gen Y, an image of young boys and girls in their school uniform, neatly seated at their desks in school. They are the future orchestrators of their country. They are the silent generation, quietly waiting for their time to shine in the international community. They are defying predefined dogma by creating their own culture that deviates from the traditions of their parents toward a Western culture with Chinese characteristics. Such a culture, comparable to the current atmosphere in China, is a fusion between communism's emphasis of the society and capitalism's emphasis of the individual.

The awakening of the generation is occurring at a rapid pace and through the means described in later chapters of this book. This culture of Gen Y is not yet set in stone; it can and will change over time. It is to the West's and the rest of the world's advantage and duty to acquaint themselves with this generation, for their thoughts and reactions to current trends and influences will have great implications for not only the future of China, but that of the world. Before the West knows it, China's Gen Y will bring their country to a new dawn that will make Westerners question their preconceptions about their own futures.

Notes

[1] http://www.economist.com/countries/China/

[2] http://news.bbc.co.uk/1/hi/technology/4263525.stm

[3] http://news.lifestyle.co.uk/technology/8832-technology.htm

[4] http://news.bbc.co.uk/1/hi/technology/4263525.stm

[5] http://news.com.com/Cell+phone+use+surges+in+China/2100-1039_3-5227836.html

[6] http://www.theregister.co.uk/2004/07/02/china_text_snoop/

[7] *International Herald Tribune*, Aug.ust 2, 2004. Front page.

[8] *International Herald Tribune*, August. 2, 2004.

[9] http://www.china.org.cn/english/China/78063.htm; http://news.bbc.co.uk/2/hi/asia-pacific/1511342.stm)

[10] http://news.bbc.co.uk/2/hi/asia-pacific/3587838.stm

[11] http://www.guardian.co.uk/china/story/0,7369,1135066,00.html

[12] Jun Jing, 2000, p. 2

[13] http://www.lclark.edu/~econ/China.htm

[14] http://www.washingtonpost.com/ac2/wp-dyn/A77925-2001May25)

[15] http://www.washingtonpost.com/ac2/wp-dyn/A77925-2001May25

[16] Jun Jing, 2000, pp. 14-15

[17] Data and statistics from China's National Bureau of statistics and verified by N-Dynamic Research and Consultancy, Shanghai.

[18] Both http://www.china.org.cn/english/2003/Feb/56198.htm and statistics from N-Dynamic Research in Shanghai.

[19] Asiaweek.com. WTO article, March 30, 2001.

[20] http://www.china.org.cn/english/2000/Oct/2966.htm

[21] http://english.people.com.cn/200403/01/eng2004 0301_136213.shtml

[22] http://english.people.com.cn/200404/22/eng20040422_141279.shtml

[23] http://www.china.org.cn/english/2003/Feb/56198.htm

[24] http://news.bbc.co.uk/1/hi/health/1860453.stm and http://www.chinatoday.com/data/data.htm

[25] http://www.concordmonitor.com/apps/pbcs.dll/article?AID=/20041203/REPOSITORY/412030315/1013/NEWS03

Chapter 3

Lifestyles of a Generation

Lifestyles have drastically evolved in China since the economic reforms of the 1980s. China's youth, specifically those in bustling urban areas, are enthusiastically accepting the foreign influence their parents once fought to isolate. The Chinese regime even appears to be supportive of modern lifestyles and new objects used to promote them. The emerging similarities between China and the West ultimately mark a new generation in China.

It is particularly of interest to notice the number of choices China's Generation Y has for its free time and entertainment. In the past, individuals were fully subject to the will of higher powers, such as family and the government; but recently this has changed with economic growth, new technologies, and new entertainment forms. This transformation is indicative of China's transition from a planned economy to a consumer economy in which teenagers, instead of their government and parents, enthusiastically make their own individual decisions. This change should not be looked on lightly, considering its clash with traditional Chinese culture.

Free time is precious to many Gen Yers, as school is a significant limiting factor. Most teenagers in my study mentioned that they have three to four hours a day (including lunch) for leisure activities, while most spend eight hours a day at school. Lifestyles are the first indicators of who the teenagers in the generation are and the direction in which they are going.

Music

You hear it on television shows, on MTV, and in the loud discotheques on city streets. More and more, music is penetrating the daily lives of China's Gen Y through media and music electronics. Already, pop music and Rhythm and Blues (R&B) have become extremely popular among the youth. A significant number of teenagers are defying their parents' career wishes and choosing the occupations of DJ (disc jockey) or musical artist. The extent of the change highlights the truly large-scale developments shaking China at the moment.

Until China made lasting reforms in the government, music and other art forms were trivialized and viewed by Mao Zedong as harmful to the state—so much so, in fact, that he left cultural institutions at the mercy of the Red Guards. Yet music is making a monumental comeback.

The popularity of music can easily be seen in karaoke bars centered in China's mega cities. Most Gen Yers sing karaoke with their friends on a regular basis. The teenagers stated that they go with about five of their friends to karaoke bars such as KTV (a very popular karaoke chain in Shanghai), Big Echo, Holiday, Cashbox, Mai Di Sheng, and Kirin to "relieve stress," especially during the treacherous entrance exam season. Karaoke is now a hobby for Gen Y, and an inexpensive and widely available one at that. A teen can sit with his or her friends at Mai Di Sheng Karaoke for an unbelievably cheap price—19 RMB ($2.30) per person for three hours. These establishments generally cater to a younger generation and sell alcohol because of the lack of a drinking age in China. In contrast, American teenagers will have trouble entering the few establishments offering karaoke because of age restrictions. In addition, peer pressure makes many Americans too nervous to sing or unwilling to endure the sight of numerous drunks making fools of themselves, even if they can legally drink alcohol.

50

Karaoke is more important than just providing stress relief. It is the youth that have largely accelerated the popularity of karaoke, because karaoke as we know it was introduced to China from Japan less than 20 years ago.[1] Further, in other Asian cultures, especially Japan and Hong Kong, karaoke bars are an imperative setting for businesspeople in making a deal; the candid interaction relieves tension and alleviates any possible skepticism between both parties making a deal. As a morphing new business culture similar to Japan's, China's business culture will absorb karaoke bars, requiring Westerners to sing with their counterparts if a deal is to be made. Western artists are targeting the youth with large concert tours. Recently, Alicia Keys (U.S.) toured China, starting in Beijing, and donated the profits to the China Youth Development Foundation.[2] Britney Spears thought the market large enough for her to plan a five-city concert tour in Beijing, Guangzhou, Shanghai, Changsha, and Shenyang in September 2004. Whitney Houston sang in front of fans in both Shanghai and Beijing in July 2004. Mariah Carey and Sarah Brightman have also performed in China.[3]

But America cannot proclaim its hegemony over music in China because Chinese teenagers overwhelmingly prefer American-style pop and R&B music from Asian origins, mostly Hong Kong and Taiwan. Chinese hip-hop moguls, such as Jay Zhou, Leehom Wang, Pan Wei Bo, Chris Yu, Sammi Cheng (Hong Kong) and Lin Jun Jie are the most popular artists. Taiwan's Jay Zhou especially wows his young fans with his wide array of music, ranging from rap and hip-hop to soul. His face is the symbol for Pepsi in China, and is posted around popular shopping centers in urban areas. One female teenager actually went to see Nicholas Tse, a famous Hong Kong singer and director, in concert. Zhou and Tse are reputed to be heartthrobs to teenage females because of their looks and sensitive style of music. Others mentioned were Tao Zhe, who combines pop with rock and symphony, and Zhou Jielun from Taiwan. Another female with different tastes in music preferred Chen Huilin (Hong Kong) and

Liang Jingru (Malaysia) for their faster rhythms. An older female preferred the love songs of Fan Xiao Xuan. One male listens to Tao Tu's hip-hop music, while another said he listened to Backstreet Boys, a band to which today's American teenage males would usually not admit listening. Music continues to evolve—rapidly—in China. Late in 2004, over 40,000 young people, half of whom from Beijing and Xi'an, traveled to Mount Helan in West China for a Woodstock-inspired rock concert of 18 national rock artists, including Cui Jian, the most famous Chinese pioneer of rock music.[4]

Generation Y is so unconventional that they have been deemed by its traditional society and various media as being rebellious, shunning the last vestiges of Chinese culture for American heavy metal.[5] Actually, this does not seem to be the case. Few teens listen to hard metal rock, although each has one friend or more who listens to such music. "Angry" music, as they call it, is loud and cacophonous for many teenagers, but it provides respite to some students before taking exams.

Have you ever heard of heavy metal?

Zhang: I know it. A lot of girls in my class like it.

Do you like it?

Zhang: Not a lot. Once in music class a student introduced it and played some. Listening to it occasionally is OK. But these girls say they listen to it all day at home, no problem. I said if I listened all day, I would go crazy.

So why do those girls prefer this kind of music?

Zhang: Maybe it has to do with their personalities, or maybe it has to do with their families. One of my classmates, since she was little…a lot of things happened to her. Her relationship with her mom and dad is not good, and maybe their family life is not very harmonious. Maybe she sometimes needs a release, and she can get it from this music.

You think it's her individuality?

Zhang: Individuality? What is unique about her is that she is a sloppy and careless type of girl. She normally talks real loud, and is really extroverted.

Gu Y. also finds this type of music to be helpful to relax prior to taking an entrance exam. This mature teen cannot help but shake his head when he hears screaming and loud rhythm. Another male said that he does not like the music, but that his friend loves it and downloads it off the Internet for free on his new broadband cable line. That music, in his eyes, is popular mainly in Europe and America, not in China.

Already on Chinese television are musical shows and music videos. MTV has established its base in Guangdong (near Hong Kong) and has sold some of its programs to over 300 cities nationwide. MTV has also created the "MTV Style Awards," which are presented to famous pop and movie stars in one big ceremony in front of nearly 120 million households.[6] Chinese television also has music programs for Gen Y's parents and grandparents. One program shows older females singing and dancing to historical Chinese tunes; this is the government's way of honoring the elderly and giving them something to do. Also, the Music Channel (Channel V), available in many locations throughout China, offers similar programming.

The successful penetration of music is illustrated by the teens' career preferences. A truly astonishing number of respondents acknowledged that they would like to pursue careers in music, such as a disc jockey (DJ) or musical artist. Chinese teenagers look at music as a form of expression often missing in their lives. It is a form of "individuality," explained Cui Jian, China's first and foremost rock star; he contested a claim by older journalists that rock music was merely a reminder of the colonial days and not a part of Chinese culture.[7] Gen Y's music is less angry and politically vocal because of the stability of the nineties, incorporating more optimistic and patriotic undertones praising youth's right to economic prosperity and a modern life. For instance, in Ai Jing's song, "I'm Made in China," she sings, "I'm made in China / they say that China's really backward; I'm made in China / they say that China's getting better..."

Tao Zhe of Taiwan, a favorite singer of Gen Y, released an album entitled *Times of Peace and Prosperity* that sold nearly 900,000 copies in its opening week.[8] His popularity stems from his direct communication with the modern generation and its confidence. Furthermore, Sun Nan, another famous pop star, believes that listeners enjoy his music because of its optimism and its celebration of China's modern era, such as its economy and lifestyle. Sun Nan captures the spirit of Gen Y: "The last generation represented a certain time, a certain set of circumstances. We don't share the old way of looking at things."[9] Although Gen Y's music in the 21st century is the happy, optimistic pop music without the blatantly angry undertones of rock and grunge music, there remains, as one teen points out, "a sense of helplessness" over problems in Chinese society.

MP3 players (MP "sun") are the major medium by which teenagers listen to their music. The teenagers have essentially skipped listening to music on CD players and have progressed toward digital music technology. MP3 players contain digital music files that are transferred from a personal computer, eliminating the need for compact discs. American and European MP3 manufacturers have trouble appealing to China's Generation Y because Korean and Japanese brands are far more high-tech, attractive, and inexpensive. The rapid ascendancy of MP3 players has exacerbated music piracy problems because listeners are ever more prone to downloading music illegally off the Internet.

Piracy has been one of the largest inhibitors of a large-scale media market developing in China. Only a few of the respondents mentioned that they shop at music stores and websites, yet many conspicuously wore MP3 players attached to their mobile phones and clothing. Gen Y has access to all of the alleyways and shops that sell inexpensive DVDs and music CDs. Internet websites and P2P (People to People) file-sharing downloading allow millions to share music via the Web. American media companies complain that they lose $2.5 billion annually in revenue and that nearly 90 percent of Chinese purchases of American media are pirated.[10] This has not only aggravated the American media industry, but also the U.S. Congress and the Bush administration, which have vowed to contest China's weak enforcement of copyright laws in front of the World Trade Organization, threatening to impose tariffs on Chinese products. Chinese artists also suffer from increased censorship and minimal exposure in state-run television outlets.[11] In addition, the Chinese government has even been known to intentionally regulate the prices of albums to decrease artists' profits.

Despite the hurdles, the future of the music industry in China is optimistic as more and more artists begin to saturate the market. Hip-hop and R&B artists from Taiwan and Hong Kong and, to a lesser degree, the U.S. will continue to entertain Gen Y until the music genre dies out, as rock and grunge did in China. Some Gen Yers will also become artists of Western-style music as seen through their dreams of becoming DJs and music artists. The growing music industry is allowing many Gen Yers to start careers in music and establish the venues and services to present music events. Judging from the musical advertising of Pepsi, we know that music advertisements and singer endorsements provide an important outlet today for reaching the youth of China. Even some fast-food restaurants bolster the popularity of Chinese pop with American characteristics and their own reputations with music on television screens. The new trends in music are illustrative of not only Western influences permeating China, but also China's transition to a consumerist economy. Teens mentioned that they listen to music to relax and to have fun. But music may have a greater significance than pleasing today's youth. It is also indicative of China's transition from a producer economy to a consumer economy because the youth now feel the need to be pleased, satisfied, and relaxed. Further,

Generation Y now chooses its entertainment and genre of music, both of which are characteristic of a consumer economy. Don't expect the underlying themes in pop music, such as relaxation, patriotism, modern living, optimism, and wealth, to cease in the near future as long as China continues to modernize.

Cartoons

Superheroes, love, mystery, and sex—such are the topics of the many comics and cartoons that China's Generation Y reads. Cartoons are an extremely popular medium among the youth. Even young professional adults can't get enough cartoons to read. One online poll by netease.com states that nearly 63 percent of Chinese young professionals read pictorials instead of books, and 70 percent of them read cartoons.[12] Almost all Chinese youth prefer Japanese cartoons, another contrast with Generation Y in America.

Perhaps one reason for the wide interest in cartoons stems from China's ostensible lack of a stigma associated with cartoons among both the youth and adults. On the other hand, Americans generally view cartoons as juvenile and babyish. For example, on the MTV reality show *Tail Daters*, one female rummaged through a male's belongings where she found his comic collection. She responded by deeming the male an immature geek and made fun of him on national television. That is the kind of message Western popular culture sends out to teenagers. The American stigma is well taken because most of the cartoons in Western animation are geared toward juveniles instead of to the general population.

The Japanese cartoons are dissimilar to American comics in that their plots cater to all ages. The content of Japanese anime is famed for including sex and violence, yet fit for an all-age audience.[13] Moreover, the cartoons' appearances are very different, for supernatural creatures often interact with human heroes. Human characters usually have unrealistic hair colors and large eyes of green, purple, and blue. And, unlike in American and European cartoons, Japanese cartoons concentrate on the movement of the face instead of the body. Similar to what Asian parents teach their children, the Japanese comics emphasize responsibility and culpability in their characters. The theme of a Japanese cartoon often centers around the character, instead of the events that are handed to him or her, as in American cartoons.

American comics and cartoons generally concentrate on dimensionality, movement, and detail; they make many more movements than Japanese cartoons. Disney cartoons are often life-like with three-dimensionality, accurate architecture, and body characteristics. A famous exception to this style is the incredibly popular American cartoon *The Simpsons*, which purposefully portrays human characters with four-fingered hands and oddly shaped bodies. Additionally, new cartoons such as *South Park, Family Guy,* and *King of the Hill* also defy the perception of the juvenility of cartoons with their inclusion of humorous social and satirical situations.

In China, girls and boys often prefer different types of cartoons. Males often prefer Boys' Anime and girls generally prefer the softer Girls' Anime. Tim, my home-stay brother, explained the differences between male cartoons and female cartoons: Boys' cartoons deal with competition and struggle, whereas girls' comics center on human relationships. Viewers watch cartoons geared toward them on Channel Young and other local stations. China's teens overwhelmingly preferred Japanese cartoons to American cartoons. American cartoons are, as one teen contends, "too far removed" from the lives of Chinese people. He suggested that Japanese people and Chinese people are quite similar, and thus "Japanese cartoons feel better." Paradoxically, the Chinese teenagers prefer entertainment and brands (mentioned later) from a country they bitterly despise; they are as bitter and unforgiving as their parents about the Japanese massacre in Nanjing during World War II.

Erotic comics are coming of age. In 2004, one erotic comic magazine offered 100,000 RMB in a contest for the best erotic cartoons; it sold 50,000 copies that month. Although the magazine meant its audience to be young professionals, many of the sales came from middle school students, or close to the Generation Y age range.[14]

In all probability, cartoons and comics, similar to computer gaming, are not only enticing because of their interesting plots, but also because they open up a virtual world away from the reality teenagers want to escape. Cartoons allow children to watch emotional relationships and interactions between men and free heroes who battle dangerous creatures, a far stretch from their overprotected lives. Cartoons will, in all probability, remain popular as the youth mature into young adults.

COSPLAY, or Costume Playing, has quickly become a popular trend in China since leaving Japan, captivating male and female young people. It is a big contest in which people dress up in costumes of their favorite cartoons or movie actors. Groups of females or males often go to these COSPLAY contests to relax. *Beijing Youth Daily* found that nearly 34 percent of the players were 15-20.[15] Part of the allure for cartoon connoisseurs is the creative and interesting building up of a character and living out that character's life without parental restrictions.

Computers

Computers are among the signature toys of China's Gen Y. History books will remember the computer as having revolutionized a generation and forever affecting its future. Whereas parents had the plain plow, Gen Y has the versatile computer. With the computer, teenagers all over the world are susceptible to trends at the click of a button.

Computer literacy for China's Gen Y is widespread, as many Gen Yers in urban areas are prone to hold jobs in Information Technology and other high-tech fields. Students learn about computers at school, and leisure activities often center around it. All teens in my study had access to computers, and the majority of them had computers at home.

Gen Y's use of the computer:

"I use the computer to type homework, and then to print. Then I can chat, chat on QQ,[16] or else go online to search for some materials."—Jiang Q.

"Sometimes I play online games, chat on QQ, things like that."—Tao

Teenagers who do not have computers go to Internet cafés to fulfill their Web needs. The popularity of Internet cafés is illustrated in numbers; on a weekend, for example, it is easy to see these locations swamped by young men and women sending e-mails, blogging, and, most often, playing games via the Web. When asked what the older male teens did for fun, the first answer blurted out of the mouth of one humorous teen was "Going to the Internet café." Computers are especially important to teenage males, who can easily spend up to four hours each day despite their homework load.

The Internet is probably the most used form of entertainment for Chinese youth next to gaming. Inexpensive Internet cafés are spreading to rural areas in China and becoming increasingly popular. Just like American teenagers, the Chinese youth use the Internet to chat online, for online courses and research, to surf, and to play games with their friends—even virtual friends courtesy of chat rooms. More teens get their news by means of the Internet than by television. This preference is illustrated by figures that show more people now purchase computers than televisions.[17]

In response to a question about the three most important aspects in her life, one female teenager included the computer in addition to family and the Internet. She was not alone. Closer interviews revealed that computers often have a greater use than what meets the eye. Computers are often the devices through which Generation Y can relax, socialize, and deal with—or escape from—their problems.

One consulting company in China contends that China will be the second largest computer market in 2006, and estimates that computer sales will increase at an average of 18.8 percent until 2007.[18] The Chinese purchased the most computers in Asia: 15 million desktops in 2004, 15 percent higher than in 2003.[19] Clearly, computers—not the plow, as some Americans are led to believe—are in the future of China.

The Internet

The Internet is becoming more essential and prolific in the lives of China's Gen Y. At the time of this writing, China boasted an Internet population of nearly 80 million people. At these rates, Mandarin will become the major language of the Internet in the future. China's youth demonstrate their enthusiasm for the Internet with a fervor not present in the U.S. or Europe.

With heightened school stress, no siblings, and demanding parents, it is no wonder that some teenagers seek solitude and/or companionship on the Internet. Through the Internet, China's youth are opening themselves up to new, unprecedented elements that are bringing them closer to the outside world and inevitably distancing them from their country's past. The government has recognized the Internet's power to do such things and has enacted numerous precautions to safeguard itself from the ostensibly corrupted youth.

The prevalence of Internet users among respondents is substantial, as 100 percent of older males and 88 percent of younger females have access. Further, the amount of usage and the importance of the Internet differ between sexes and age groups. Such differences, noticed by the teens themselves, have led to some of their ideas about gender, such as girls working harder because they focus on their studies more than they play on computers.

Teenagers enjoy viewing new Web pages with interesting designs. Humorous cartoons using loud colors like red, orange, and yellow catch their attention. Remember, the Internet is where this generation spends huge amounts of their time; they have the right to be picky about the design of Web pages.

There are tons of sites aimed at the youth, both in Chinese and English. One major site is Ynet, which offers many news outlets such as *China Youth Daily* and *Beijing Youth Daily* as well as blogs and forums. Blogs are often the best means to find out what is perplexing the quiet youth, yet these sites are by no means a totally free speech medium. In red ink, the Ynet's blog prohibits publishing decadent, reactionary, violent, or personal attack articles.

Yahoo.com, 163.com (Netease), Baidu.com (a search engine), Battle.net for Internet gaming, and Cnemu.com are among the group's favorites. Increasingly popular is the Shanghai F1 website for F1 news and Sohu.com and Sina.com.cn, two major Web portals, for general news. These sites provide the youth with BBS (Bulletin Board System) pages, which allows them to carry on conversations with other people in Internet forums and blogs.[20] They use the Internet for information, online courses, entertainment news, chatting (on QQ), e-mail, Web surfing for enjoyment, and "to play games occasionally," such as the game Miracle (MU) for 2-3 hours per session and 5-10 hours during the weekend.

Half of the younger males turn on their Web browsers as soon as they get home from school, and it is not too uncommon for them to use the Internet as much as 12 hours a day on the weekend, by far the longest time span of any group. Older boys spend four to five hours per day on the Internet and upward of six to seven hours per weekend day. They use the Internet for research, playing games, reading news, and chatting. Gen Y also

downloads music and argues that the Internet enriches their extracurricular life.

What else do you do besides chat when you are online?

Wang & Xu W.: Play games.

Zhan: Watch movies.

Xu J.: Download some songs. I also view my school alumni online.

All: News.

Wang J.: If you want to communicate with your friends, you can chat with a group of people through the Internet. If you make a phone call, you can only contact them one by one. If you go online, you can talk with all of them.

The younger males have become very Internet savvy and spend anywhere from one hour to three hours a day on it. Males employ the Internet more than usual, but that does not have any significant effect on their lives. Females use the Internet at school, Internet cafés, their home or their friends' home to download music, chat, and play games—though their time, usually 1-3 hours a day, is limited because of school obligations.

How do Gen Yers justify their Internet usage to their parents? The youth have found a way to appeal to their parents' dreams of success by relating their Internet usage to the amount of success they will have in the future. Others have trouble justifying hours and hours on the Internet, and some admitted they prefer outside activities. One younger male admitted that he favors sports over the Internet, contending that the Internet is not healthy because in his mind it inhibits human development. His view is probably that of his parents and grandparents. Two others believed that teenagers should not be cooped up inside glaring at computer screens. In spite of these opposing views, the Internet has become a daily routine for the vast majority of Gen Y teens.

It is difficult to fathom how the Internet cannot influence the teenagers' lives if they spend so much time on it. The teenagers claim that they are able to live without the Internet; however, those same teenagers would not know how to keep themselves occupied were they deprived of it.

"I'm Afraid I'll Be Cheated"

Although Gen Yers do not purchase a lot online, they still learn about products. As they become more comfortable and convinced on the safety of e-commerce, Gen Yers will eventually buy online. The male teens are more willing to buy online than the girls, purchasing joysticks, books, computer games, food takeout, and CDs. Teenagers judge the safety of sites by name recognition and the reputation of the sites from which they purchase, and thus will mostly purchase from sites such as Yahoo and NetEase.com.

There are close to 80 million Internet users, and the fastest growing segment of users is the teenager. Usage of the Internet among China's youth is blossoming, making it apparent that those marketers who want to target their products and services toward this segment will have to develop multi-channel approaches (e.g., stores, catalogs, websites, etc.). A study conducted by InterMedia of Washington, D.C., found that the Web-surfing community in China has more than doubled in the years from 2000 to 2002. The study, which included the results of 8,122 interviewed consumers 15 years of age and older, found that six out of ten of these Internet users were under the age of 30. Only 62 percent of study respondents had secondary education, indicating the Internet's accessibility to even wider audiences. The most popular place to access the Web was at Internet cafés, followed by the user's home.

The use of remote access locations for Internet use continues to increase throughout China, led by none other than McDonald's.[21] Last year, McDonald's installed wireless "hot spots" in many of its restaurants in Guangzhou and other locations, allowing its mostly young customers who have laptops and other digital devices to grab e-mail and surf the Web free of charge.

The study uncovered the major uses for the Internet in China, finding that two-thirds of the respondents use the Internet for gaming, exceeding e-mail usage by 10 percent. The second major activity for the Internet was to obtain the latest news from sites that are accessible, except Radio Free Asia, which the government restricts. The following chart summarizes how the InterMedia respondents use the Internet.[22]

How Do You Use the Internet?	
To Play Games	64%
To Find the Latest News	58%
To Play Music	58%
For Chat Rooms	54%
To Send/Receive E-Mail	46%
To Download Software	37%
For Work-Related Activities	22%

Source: InterMedia.org

Note: Percentage exceeds 100 because it is a multiple-choice survey.

The InterMedia study underscores how primed the teenage markets in China are for electronic games and other forms of Web-based entertainment, including services that allow them to grab news and songs off the Internet. The numbers indicate that the Internet has made even greater leaps in early adoption rates among China's youth than their counterparts in many Westernized nations because the Internet is replacing newspapers and other forms of media, such as radio, television, and even compact discs.

The popularity of the Internet among the youth has certainly caused problems in traditional Chinese society. Experts have cautioned adults about the existence of a condition known as "Internet Syndrome" that threatens their children. Doctor Yu Haiting, vice-president of a hospital in Zhengzhou, Henan province, diagnosed a patient with a mental health syndrome in which the patient was found talking to herself and her boyfriend in cyberspace after playing on the Internet for many days on end. She is not alone, for another teen was diagnosed with a mental disorder after having Web-surfed for six hours a day for five years. His symptoms, including lowered grades, altered communication with his parents and relatives, and his belief that he was being watched by the Internet, are not too much different from the symptoms of some of the new patients Dr. Yu claims to see weekly. The doctor has urged parents to restrict Internet use by children and teenagers, who in his eyes are particularly susceptible, and recommend them to have more communication with the outside world.[23] The story indicates the fears some parents in China have of the Internet's ability to corrupt Generation Y.

The government is using heavy Internet use as a means to shut down Internet cafés. Since 2003, the government has launched a major movement to enforce a law that restricts the patronage of people under the age of 18 by sending inspectors to monitor Internet cafés and forbidding them from sprouting up within a 200-meter radius of residences and schools. The General Administration for Industry and Commerce (GAIC) says that Internet cafés have corrupted the youth by their diffusion of information and negative influence on the grades of teenagers, and that the effort is purely a means to ensure the proper moral development of the youth. [24] The government's movement was in response to several deaths that occurred because of the Internet, including those of two teenagers who evidently fell asleep on train tracks after heavy Internet usage, and twenty-five university students who perished when a fire engulfed an unprepared Internet café. The government shut down 47,000 Internet cafés in 2004 and only recognizes 90,000 that are legal, though the actual number is significantly larger.[25]

The Internet poses a threat to the government as Internet blogs, or electronic message boards, become popular tools for university students. Students often use blogs for game cheats, advice, potential services, and, increasingly, their opinions. It is worth mentioning that blogs played a major role as a battleground for both political parties during the U.S. Presidential Election of 2004 because they allowed anybody with a computer to give his or her opinion to the world on an issue.

The government's decision further illustrates the paradox confronting the government. It wants students to keep pace with the Internet revolution, but fears that total Web freedom would make the Internet a channel to spread unfavorable political ideas. The youth see Beijing tightening its grip over their Web activities through draconian measures that further divide urban Internet culture and traditional society.

Not only does the Internet's rapid dissemination of information of all kinds threaten the government, but it also threatens traditional family life by taking away precious time from family bonding. Parents have noticed their children's insatiable demand for the Internet. Although parents complain about this new influence and its power over their children, they are the ones who bring the device into their homes and readily cater to their children's requests. As long as their children maintain their grades and use their Internet skills to aid them in obtaining a job in the future, they generally allow their children to play on the computer. Family bonding will be compromised for many families, but it will not disintegrate.

Computers and the Internet are the best methods for reaching the youth market in China, for they ensure a greater audience than do all other media.

Console Gaming

Console and PC gaming are both extremely popular forms of recreation for Gen Y. PC gaming is defined as games made to play on a personal computer. PC games can easily be pirated, unlike gaming consoles such as Sony Playstation® or Microsoft Xbox. Many Internet sites offer free game downloads to entice players to buy the authentic game. In order to play console games, one needs to buy the console (usually $125), purchase controllers, and link the console and controllers to a television.

Qin, a teenage male, remarked that unlike the majority of his friends who play games on the Internet, he only enjoys playing games on his PC. Several other teenagers, including my home-stay brother, agreed with him, preferring to play games alone rather than play with Internet users from around the world. As they explained, some games are better fit for personal use. Popular PC games in China are *Warcraft*, *Starcraft*, and *Counterstrike*, among other Japanese games. *Warcraft* is a game in which players around the world embark on an errant journey to kill monsters. Even my home-stay brother enjoyed playing *Counterstrike* and *Warcraft* at home and at his friends' homes. These games are also sold in the United States, but do not have the same popularity as in China.

Console games generally are more popular in the United States than in China. Only one teen in my study wanted to buy a Nintendo Game Boy Advance. One possible reason for this is that console games are more expensive and difficult to find. Furthermore, the console companies, such as Sony, Sega, Nintendo, and Microsoft, do not enjoy selling products in China because the nation is well known for its proclivity for pirated goods.

67

Internet Gaming

Internet gaming, as opposed to software console gaming, allows teenagers and adults to compete online against Internet friends in their favorite games. Internet gaming is all the rage in China: nearly 14 million people have played Internet games. The future is bright for these games, as new players are expected to increase by 50 percent yearly over the next five years.[26]

"Everybody plays them (Internet games)," said a male referring to the popularity of Internet games. In fact, only three males in my study mentioned that they do not enjoy gaming. The interest of all other boys in games ranges from minor hobby to fanatical fervor. Zhang explains the difference between males and females regarding spending their time:

Boys' time outside of class is different from girls', who can go out shopping. Boys like to stay in groups. If they're not playing sports, they're on the computer. Maybe in the summertime when it's hot or whatever, they're not willing to go out, so they stay in the house and play games.

Females also play Internet games, but to a lesser degree. Two played *Mo Li Bao Bei,* or *Cross Gate,* in their spare time. Part of the allure of the game was that it allowed them to make friends with other players, in addition to the captivating fantasy world they illustrate. Another female plays *Legend of Mir,* a game similar to *Warcraft,* although it takes place in a "mysterious oriental-style world"[27] where players can hone their Taoist spiritual values to battle creatures. Games specifically aimed at Asian youth such as *Legend of Mir* may do better in the long run because Chinese teenagers relate better to Asian media.

A player can connect through a pay-to-play website such as Sohu.com. More and more, teens are using free gaming software on websites made by ordinary Internet junkies and downloading free demos and redownloading them after they expire.

All of you will play the trial edition first, won't you?

All: Agree.

Jiang: I once downloaded a trial edition of the game *Rune II*. Now we can find the formal edition of this game, and it only costs around 68 RMB. But at the time I downloaded it, it was connected to a foreign website and cost 2 RMB for every MB. In the end, I paid more than 300 RMB.

Many unfamiliar with the gaming world, including the parents of Gen Y, may not understand the causes for such gaming mania and therefore need to know several reasons for the games' popularity. First, the popularity of Internet gaming is commensurate with that of television in America during the 1950s because, unlike television today, so much has yet to be discovered on the Internet. Secondly, through electronic games teenagers have the capability of creating a *free*, simulated character who faces exciting dangers in an alluring fantasy world different from their Chinese society known to shun individual freedom. Many of the games have colorful and unique settings that are a far stretch from the lives they live. Thirdly, the provocative games provide an escape for hours on end from parental interaction and the unrelenting pressures of school.

Gaming is also an easy way to make friends. One male explained that he had two types of friends: his school friends and his Internet gaming friends. He clearly distinguished between the two by stating that with his Internet friends he was able to tell his personal secrets and ask for their advice. He believed his friends at school were more concerned with their own well-being and only spoke about schoolwork and computer games. He mentioned that his biggest fear was that his Internet friends would betray his trust and expose his secrets. This teenager's method of communication resembles a larger problem in Generation Y, since other males and females made the same distinction. Some teenagers are turning to computers in search of friends and advice on personal secrets rather than openly socialize in the real world. Internet friendships are difficult to maintain outside of the Internet café because of the inherent security problems, of which China's youth are aware.

The extent to which the youth have fallen for such games is impressive. Much of their free time and disposable money are absorbed by games. Some teenagers spend the whole weekend at Internet cafés. Teenagers have already decided to join the virtual reality by altering their career preferences and preferred living destinations. Not only are the games taking away their crucial study time, but the virtual reality is also creating problems for society. Eclipsed by both school and individual indulgence on the computer, Gen Y's communication skills lack in comparison with those of their peers in many parts of the world. It is apparent that a considerable number of these teenagers I studied are extremely coy and unable to assert themselves in a conversation compared to their Western counterparts, largely due to their lack of verbal communication caused by gaming and the Internet. Parents and government alike are responding by restricting access to Internet gaming, feeling that corruption will ensue and grades will fall.

Sports

In China, teens seem to enjoy playing sports as much as they watch sports. Their love for sports may be rooted in the conservative nature of the Chinese society, for sports, unlike Internet gaming, are time-honored hobbies that not only unite a community but also enhance individual thinking and health. It is no wonder that my conservative home-stay family was far more passionate about sports than about Internet gaming. In the Chinese school system, physical education is viewed by students and parents as a vital subject, and Chinese teenagers would be stunned to learn that physical education is not required in some schools in the United States.

Chinese male teens are predominantly fascinated with basketball and its professional players, especially Michael Jordan and Yao Ming, the famous Chinese basketball star who plays in the NBA. Soccer is also a very common sport to both males and females, as most have access and can easily play on the soccer fields of local schools. My home-stay brother particularly loved soccer; he frequently updated me on the outcome of the Asia Cup soccer game during my stay in Shanghai. He informed me that the Shanghainese youth are particularly sportive and generally prefer athletic products to other goods. Surprisingly growing in popularity are tennis, bowling, and badminton, which currently has a large following because it is taught at school.

As for Chinese girls, they like to play badminton, ping-pong, and basketball as well as swim and dance. Several females, in line with Zhang X.'s comments below, mentioned that they are particularly athletic.

You mentioned that you are training now. Is that soccer?

Zhang: Right, soccer.

Why do you like soccer?

Zhang: One reason is that I inherited it from my mom and dad, who are both good at sports, and my gym grade is good. Then, when I was in elementary school, I was chosen by the school to practice with the district team. I have been playing since I was in third grade.

That's already quite a few years.

Zhang: Already seven or eight.

Do you really like it? Or do you think you might quit?

Zhang: At the beginning…actually, when I was preparing for the high school entrance exam, I thought about quitting, but every time I talked to my dad about it the conversation was so hard that I stopped bringing it up. Before, my dad never agreed, but once he said, "Whatever you want." At

71

that time even if I really wanted to quit, I don't think I would have if I thought more about it.

You couldn't give it up. It's already a part of your life.

Zhang: Right, you could say that.

China is known for its obsession with biking. If the teenagers are too busy to play sports, some fulfill their thirst for exercising by biking, an important means of transportation to school and work, for about ten to fifteen minutes each trip. Wealthy families will often spoil their kids with expensive bikes, providing the lucky owners with a reason to brag at the school lunch table.

When they are not playing or watching hoops, some teenagers have gone or wish to go camping with their friends and families in various locations throughout China. Yang M., 16 years old, went with his friends to the Oriental Oasis, a camping spot for teenagers in Shanghai's Zhujiajiao Industrial and Economic Zone on the outskirts of the city, and to the suburbs with his friends. My home-stay brother went with his parents to Hainan Island, China's Hawaii in Southern China, while a female teen went with her parents to Suzhou, China's Venice of the East. One friend of mine even went camping with her friends at the Great Wall and slept on a not-yet-renovated part closed to the public. It is expected that Gen Yers will camp and vacation more than their parents as they gain more income and mobility.

The American NBA has left its mark among Chinese youth ever since the NBA recruited Wang ZhiZhi, the first Chinese NBA player, and Yao Ming, the NBA's No. 1 draft pick. Basketball aficionados can be seen wearing American basketball attire from Nike and reading any articles on the NBA on the Internet or in magazines. The sport has become so pervasive that there is even a professional national basketball association, the Chinese Basketball Association (CBA), which promotes the sport around China and has 43 men's and 42 women's teams.[28] Youth can also play in the KFC Championships for China's youth, which allows teenagers to play with other amateur teams and brought nearly 50,000 young fans to the games in 2004.

Another activity of interest is Formula One racing introduced to Shanghai by the West in October 2004. Although mentioned by only one female, it is steadily growing in popularity as more people in China own cars. Car racing has already made some die-hard young fans who anxiously await more events.

During the 2004 Olympics, the Chinese were ecstatic at their country's impressive accumulation of medals that placed China in second place overall, just below the U.S. The country's pride was unshakable as everybody seemingly tuned in late at night to track the wins of Chinese athletes, whereas Americans gave the Olympics much less attention. Hosting the 2008 Olympic Games in Beijing has monumental importance for the Chinese, as it truly signifies China's opening up to the world. Just as they were during the 2004 Olympics, Chinese youth are very proud of their country's athletics and demand winning medals from their Olympic athletes in Beijing.

These Western sporting events are having phenomenal success in China and will continue to be a huge marketing outlet for Western advertisers and corporations.

Television & Movies

So, why do you choose to play games on the computer?

Gu Y.: I cannot go out to have fun every day because it is not affordable for me. When I stay at home, it is so boring to watch TV. Compared to it, playing a computer game is much more interesting as long as I can choose what game I am going to play.

So it makes you feel free, right?

Gu Y.: Yes, and if I play a role in the game, I will be totally involved and forget about all my worries.

Television may be becoming less popular with the youth as computer use is becoming more widespread. Television and movies are often seen as activities that waste time. Television in China is quite different from that in the United States. First, Chinese television offers fewer channels and programs than American television. Secondly, Chinese people generally do not like to watch the same programming as their American counter-parts. Chinese television presents Kung Fu programs, documen-taries, cartoons, historical reenactments, soap operas, govern-ment-controlled news programs, and music programs—in con-trast to the American emphasis on game shows and reality se-ries. However, the youth enjoy watching syndicated American television series such as *G.I. Joe*, *Inspector Gadget*, and *Captain Planet*.

For the youth, there is a popular channel called Channel Young, which is somewhat a mix of Cartoon Network and MTV without its reality television shows and sexual innuendos. One older female mentioned that she enjoys watching *Today's Impres-sion (Jin Ri Yin Xiang)* and *Modern Times*. The Music Channel (Chan-nel V) watched by many teenagers is also surprisingly similar to American music channels, playing pop music produced locally throughout Asia and broadcasting the first Chinese music awards. Though none of the teens mentioned MTV as a channel he/she watches, MTV is building a rapidly growing empire in China through the youth.

"No time for television, too boring," Yu Q. said. He did reply, however, that when he does occasionally watch television he watches history documentaries on China Central Television (CCTV). He was not alone. Gu Y. loves the Discovery Channel's documentaries. Females generally preferred to watch Channel Young and soap operas from Japan and Korea, from which many of the trends they follow originate. One girl loves *18 Sui de Tian Kong (The Sky of the Eighteen-Year-Olds)*, a program in which teach-ers care about their students and help them with their daily prob-lems, thereby appealing to stressed-out kids. She wishes that teachers in real life would be as caring and humorous as some are in the television show.

Teenagers receive much of their knowledge about products by advertisements on television. Ads that are humorous and emphasize consumerism are very popular. The tone in advertisements now is starkly different from the commercials during the 1980s, which on the whole attempted to peddle industrial materials to farmers.[29] Advertisements also construct a mold of what it looks and feels like to be a "modern" youth, in addition to how to attain such an appearance. Moreover, foreign movies strengthen English language speaking skills for viewers. One of my friends learned to speak English quite well mainly by watching hundreds of American movies.

The cinema is geared more toward yuppies and people in their 20s. A male explains the situation best: "You must have a girlfriend to go to the movies." It is customary for couples to see a movie together at a cinema, tacitly prohibiting most Gen Yers from going there. Gu Y. only goes to the cinema with his school to see movies on Mao Zedong and Deng Xiaoping, among others.

Boys generally put up the most resistance to going to the cinema, preferring to watch movies on their laptops and at their friends' homes than in the awkward environment of the movie theater. The price of attending movies remains another obstacle to Gen Yers. The youth can and do buy pirated DVDs ($1.00 each) from stands laden with them throughout Shanghai, where they most often purchase science fiction, thrillers, action, horrors, and love flicks. Yu Q. prefers Japanese horror flicks to American ones because they are more psychological than the "gory" American films.

Zhang: Recently I saw *Day after Tomorrow*. It was pretty good—a disaster movie.

So, do you enjoy watching American movies, like Hollywood movies, or do you prefer movies of the Hong Kong type?

Zhang: If I am going to the movies to really see a movie, an American movie is better The sound is completely different at home and in the theatre. For Taiwan and Hong Kong movies, it's good enough just to buy a DVD or VCD and watch them at home.

Alleyways are laden with shops selling old and new pirated films—American, European, Japanese, Korean, and Taiwanese— giving some urban Chinese teens relatively the same, or perhaps even wider, access to movies as American teenagers. Most teenagers can name famous American movies and even television shows, such as *Sex and the City*, *The Simpsons*, and *Friends. Sex and the City* is one of the most sought after DVDs in China despite the government's ban on the show. There is even a Taiwanese version of the show on television entitled *Hot Ladies* that airs in Shanghai and Beijing, and a comic book that has sold very well on the Mainland. However, the American version is more popular because of its creative storylines and the view that it is more authentic.[30] Clearly, the lifestyle portrayed in the series is of interest to female yuppies in Shanghai and Beijing who share similar experiences with the females of the show.

Reading

Despite the rapidly rising popularity of Internet and video games, interest in reading continues to rise. One survey in 1999 on Gen Y's relationship with reading concluded that the popularity of magazines, newspapers, and Internet articles surpassed that of books, which ranked fourth in overall popularity. Surprisingly, interest in reading has remained constant in spite of the growing popularity of computerized media.

The rise in reading is a result of better living conditions due to modernization, more free time to read, and a nationwide program to increase literacy and college acceptances. An increased supply of books, aided by relaxed governmental supervision, and an increase in the number of libraries have also made more books accessible to Gen Y. Chinese youth are now more prone to read books on computers, economics, and how-to guides than to read Mao Zedong's teachings, which were required reading for Gen Y's parents in their adolescence.[31]

My research revealed a disparity between the sexes when it came to reading. Half of the older boys did not prefer reading in their spare time, in contrast to the majority of females who enjoyed reading novels, online books, and, of course, magazines. The younger males on the verge of graduation to high school read more than their elders, preferring to read news on the Internet, which helps them on their entrance exams.

In school, students read Chinese literature and world literature from the United States and Europe. Outside of school, creative martial arts or kung fu novels are in the hands of many teenagers. Yu Q. reads Jin Yong, by far the most famous author of kung fu novels, whose storylines are serialized on Chinese television. Females take the lead in reading romance novels. One female is enthralled by Zhang Xiaoxian's fantasy character "Blue Moon," who falls in love but then turns into a vampire. Many Gen Yers are accessing books in the form of e-books, which have become increasingly more common to the youth, as they are inexpensive and easy to access.

Inasmuch as Chinese students appear obsessed about success, it comes as little surprise that yuppies and young adults demand how-to and business management books. The reaction of college students and professionals in Beijing and Harbin, a northeastern city, to Chester Elton, who wrote and sold 50,000 copies of *The 24-Carrot Manager*, was similar to what an A- or B-list celebrity would expect to receive in a high school.[32] The relatively short work is a handbook of key American business practices and management tips. The author marketed his book by building hype around it, creating a style by throwing carrots into the audience, and appealing to a significant goal in the lives of millions of Chinese. Similar authors have made a killing in writing books on management and how-to-get-rich books aimed at Chinese young adults. Michael Porter of Harvard University received a similar reception. Like a music star, he presented his seminar to some spectators who paid over $1,000 for a seat. Stephen Covey, author of *The Seven Habits of Highly Effective People,* promoted his book with a Web-streaming seminar for Chinese businesspeople who paid $50,000 for his insight. The Chinese government has even hired some of these authors to give advice to Chinese companies owned by the state on how to make them more competitive. Teenagers not yet focused on management tips read how-to and instructional books that will help them plan their careers and prepare for entrance exams.

There is a great potential for books aimed at teens in their future life, especially those targeting 15- to 17-year-old females. These books need to keep their audience in mind and incorporate light tones into their themes. There is also a potential for novels about the journeys of cartoon characters through mythical lands. With the right subject matter and the right publicity, these books will surely be a success in the China market. Furthermore, as seen by Chester Elton's marketing strategy, books focusing on entrepreneurship, success, knowledge for the 21st century, and especially wealth-building have the opportunity to capture the market for older Gen Yers who hope to find wealth in China's tumultuous, competitive job market. Although China does have the state-run Xinhua Bookstore network, it needs to create a more powerful mechanism, such as a more widespread bookstore chain that allows publishers to sell their books throughout the nation.

Magazines play a major role in molding a modern Generation Y. The diffuse gaming magazines purchased by both males and females keep the youth up-to-date on changing trends and ways to keep up with them. These widespread magazines contribute to the immense popularity of games, making gaming almost a norm for teenagers. Furthermore, the trends in beauty magazines (e.g., *Nan Sheng Nü Sheng* [*Boys and Girls*] and *Ray Li*) and their advertisements on buses and signs promote the idea that Western trends are more advanced. They primarily influence females about what it looks like to be a "modern" girl, giving them a pattern to follow.

China's youth, including university students, read more than any other age segment in China and may become the largest consumers of books in the future. This zest for reading will give rise to a wider dissemination of new ideas and lead to a greater cultivation of the individual.

China's Technobrats

The technological environment surrounding China's Gen Y is increasingly becoming like that of our own. Certainly, technology is one major difference in the adolescence of Generation Y and that of the preceding generation. Already Shanghai has the first magnetic bullet train. China's mobile phone market is the largest in the world and is growing rapidly. Nearly 95 percent of urban homes have televisions.[33] Internet connectivity is exploding, and China is making strides with its space program and military. High-tech devices are already the norm for many teenagers in urban areas. Given the youth's quick adaptation to technology seen as necessary for life in a modern world, they will continue to be up-to-date with technology.

Mobile phones are all the rage to China's Generation Y, whose fondness for them is manifested through China's monolithic growth as a communications empire. China is already the largest cell phone market with 300 million users, and the percentage of people who have cell phones will soon overtake those of all developed nations combined. A large majority of teenagers mentioned they had mobile phones, and many showed off

79

their cell phones to their peers by laying them down in front of them or conspicuously attaching them to their bodies in a nonchalant fashion.

China's mobile market will be one of the most competitive markets as new mobile phones quickly replace the old. The Chinese government is investing in 3G technology, one of the most advanced forms of cell phone technology that will allow users to watch streaming video. [34]

The two major providers of cell phone services in China are China Mobile and China Unicom, which host approximately 300 million mobile phone users in both urban and rural regions.[35] Their phones run on GSM technology, the frequency that most of the world operates on, as opposed to the smaller CDMA network primarily used in North America.

China's youth are very fond of foreign mobile phone brands, especially Nokia, Sony, Siemens, Erickson, and Alcatel. Even more appealing to sellers of these products is Generation Y's purchasing power, as they spend relatively large amounts of their—or their parents'—money on cellular phones. For example, older females (17-18) will spend 1,500 to 3,000 RMB ($180-360) for a mobile phone, depending on a device's accoutrements and look.

Some domestic mobile phone brands mentioned by respondents were Dibitel, Ben-Q (Taiwan), and Bird. Gen Y only prefers high-tech mobile phones that are small, sleek, and "good-looking." When browsing to purchase a cell phone, they consider the following to be the most important factors in their decision: digital camera, recording features, internal antennae, and Internet capabilities. Internet capabilities appear to be very important to Chinese teens, more so than America's Gen Y, who often trails behind in mobile capabilities.

Among all other toys, mobile phones are a means for Gen Yers to gain bragging rights at school or for their parents to show off their newfound wealth. The lunch table during school is the locale for teens to shove their high-tech phones into their friends' faces. The sleeker, smaller, and more expensive a phone looks, the more desirable it will be. Teenagers overall replace or yearn to replace their mobiles often to keep up with the trends. Teenagers are already looking forward to 3G, the next generation of mobile technology, and are dreaming about the future when they will be able to watch movies, play more advanced games, and visibly chat with their friends on their mobiles.

When asked specifically, "What do you do for fun?" one male's reply, "Using my mobile phone," mimicked a lot of other teenagers. Young people in China love to play games on their mobiles if they are not near a computer. It is hard to talk about these Gen Yers without mentioning their high-tech cell phones, which, in addition to computers, have almost become a symbol of their identity as a generation.

Many MP3 players sold in China are now becoming more advanced than those sold in the United States. Some of the players even rival those of America, boasting dictionaries, voice recorders, FM radios, and multilanguage displays. Aigo, a Chinese manufacturer, even produces a wide variety of ergonomic accessories, such as MP3 wrist watches and MP3 sunglasses, which have an uncanny resemblance to Oakley's MP3 sunglasses. Chinese MP3 players offer very similar looks and shapes to Korean and Japanese players but at a much lower cost. I, like the teens I interacted with, had to get one of these MP3 players! I purchased mine in a department store in Beijing where most teenagers buy their electronics. MP3 players ran from $100 and up depending on the brand, origin, and size, which is often the length of an index finger and one inch thick. For about $120 and several minutes of bargaining with the shop owner, I bought a Chinese 128 MB MP3 player; and although it looked great, it broke several months later.

Shopping

OK, so on the weekend, what do you do?

Zhang X.: Go out shopping. Generally, girls like to walk around, looking at accessories. We have long hair, you know? And then stuff like necklaces. After I started high school I began to understand a bit about makeup, so sometimes I go shopping with my classmates to look at that.

Shopping for Western goods is the rage in urban centers, though shopping for many teens consists more of socializing with friends and window-shopping than the actual purchasing of expensive goods. On the whole, females shopped for clothes while males shopped for computer equipment, although both equally shopped for mobile phones, MP3s, and other electronics.

Contrary to previous generations, fashion is very important to the youth. In the times of their old-fashioned parents, clothing was a necessity and standing out was not tolerable. Now, marketers from abroad dictate shopping trends over which Gen Y has little control. A female indicated that all of her friends want to be "different" because the cool idea originated from a Japanese magazine. However, when asked why, she did not have a concrete answer. The fad of being different may just be an ideal brainwashed into them. Other ideas that originate from the West deal with individualism. Later in this book it will become apparent that the generation has greater trouble relating with their parents as a result of the new influences and information blasted into their minds on a daily basis. Despite this ostensible vulnerability to foreign trends, the teens are resigned, if not elated, at Western penetration, for only one male in the study was against the Westernization of China.

These thoughts and fads are remarkable, since the parents of Generation Y were against Western influence because they grew up during the years of Mao Zedong and the Cultural Revolution. China then was against Western trends and maintained a closed-door policy. Chairman Mao advocated the ideas of uniformity and equality, a direct contradiction of today's youth who brag and show off their more expensive MP3 players, mobile phones, and designer clothing. Now the fashion-conscious teens in China eat lunch at McDonald's, read Japanese fashion magazines, drink and dance on Beijing's Sanlitun Road, and window-shop for trendy sports clothing on Shanghai's Nanjing Road.

Shanghai now boasts shopping mall Plaza 66 that contains many high-end stores, such as Chanel and Louis Vuitton, and presents an opulent shopping environment in a glass atrium with marble, rivaling the malls of Beverly Hills. Although few can afford to buy from the stores, many end up wearing strikingly identical knockoffs. It is only the high elite who can buy from these boutiques, as prices are comparatively more expensive than in America because of customs duties and other costs necessary to sell in China. In reality, most urban teenagers in my study shop at nearby stores on streets or alleyways and in department stores.

Many of these leisure activities have either originated from or been heavily influenced by the West, highlighting the extent to which Chinese youth accept foreign influences. The new activities, in some cases the last respites from the pressurized adolescence in which they live, are there to stay in China, but in all probability their composition will morph in time, for the youth will, as they have in many other instances, put their own spin on them.

Notes

[1] http://www.karaokescene.com/history/
[2] http://www.china.org.cn/english/culture/106324.htm.
[3] http://www.china.org.cn/english/Life/101674.htm.
[4] http://www.china.org.cn/english/culture/103453.htm.

[5]http://en.chinabroadcast.cn/1857/2004-7-9/53@130284.htm.

[6]http://www.viacom.com/press.tin?ixPressRelease=80454169.

[7]Suzanne Gottschang and Lyn Jeffery, p. 82.

[8]http://enmms.chinabroadcast.cn/features/beats/0415beat.pdf.

[9]http://www.china.org.cn/english/culture/81166.htm
also the remarks of Ai Jing above.

[10]http://www.ifpi.org/site-content/antipiracy/piracy2002.html.

[11]Suzanne Gottschang and Lyn Jeffery, p. 79.

[12]http://www.chinadaily.com.cn/english/doc/2004-08/27/
content_369384.htm.

[13]http://www.honors.uiuc.edu/ealc15097/Hiten-Ivan/style.htm.

[14]http://www.chinadaily.com.cn/english/doc/2004-08/27/
content_369384.htm.

[15]http://game.china.com/zh_cn/news/news3/507/20041208/
12002595.html&prev=/ In Chinese, translated by Google.

[16]The Web portal in which many Chinese teens mentioned they chat.
See http://www.qq.com.

[17]http://www.china-embassy.org/eng/xw/t40400.htm.

[18] http://english.people.com.cn/200203/05/eng20020305_91450.shtml.

[19]http://au.news.yahoo.com/050309/19/tezf.html.

[20]http://www.google.com search?hl=en&lr=&as_qdr=all&oi
=defmore&q=define:BBS.

[21]http://www.wi-fiplanet.com/news/article.php/3084121.

[22]http://www.intermedia.org/news_and_publications/publications/
China%20and%20the%20Internet.pdf.

[23]http://www.chinadaily.com.cn/english/doc/2004-02/12/
content_305555.htm.

[24]http://www.chinadaily.com.cn/english/doc/2004-05/06/
content_328462.htm.

[25]http://english.people.com.cn/200502/25/eng20050225_174750.html
and see http://www.chinadaily.com.cn/english/doc/2004-02/12/
content_305555.htm for statistics.

[26]http://www.chinadaily.com.cn/english/doc/2004-02/16/
content_306325.htm.

[27]As described by the site running the game http://www.legendofmir.net/

[28]http://www.china.org.cn/english/features/2004-2005cba/118959.htm.

[29]Suzanne Gottschang and Lyn Jeffery, p. 176.

[30]http://news.bbc.co.uk/2/hi/entertainment/3043037.stm.

[31]http://www.honco.net/100day/02/2000-0526-liu.html, including the survey findings several paragraphs before.

[32]David Barboza, "7 Habits of Highly Effective Cadres: Western Management Experts Descend on an Eager China," *New York Times*, February 19, 2005, C1 and C3.

[33]Jun Jing, 2000, p. 19.

[34]http://www.china.org.cn/english/scitech/94703.htm.

[35]As of August 2004.

Chapter 4

Chinese Society
and the Individual

Social Relationships

What would you say are the five most important aspects of your life at present?

"Um...family, friends...what else? I can't really think of anything else to say at the moment."

Social relationships are some of the strongest influences in an individual's life and are of enormous importance to China's Generation Y because of the strong emphasis on filial piety—the obligations between children and family—in Chinese culture. Elder kin, rather than individual whims, have traditionally decided what a teenager does and what one will become. Individual roles thought up by Confucius are assigned to each individual for the benefit of the family. These rules are so specific that to be truly filial, Confucius claimed, a son must follow the goals of his father until three years after his death; and if followed properly, that son would be able to perform well his ever so important occupation. As a result of the Confucian philosophy, the Chinese look at the world and their community with a sense of "We," instead of "I." These roles are so well defined to the youth that if they go unfulfilled a family member may feel extremely uncomfortable.

It is impossible to deny that China's system of relationships has formulated or at least heavily influenced the identities of the youth. It is also difficult to deny that the relationship of youth to their parents is not one of emotional or economic dependency. The Chinese family is thus generally stronger than a Western family. While the Chinese family is more cohesive and functional as a group, it generally offers a closed family life, one that limits personal expression and interaction.

Though they are inundated each day with foreign influences and are forced to either keep or reject various aspects of tradition, Chinese youth still vow to keep close to the tenets of filial piety, believing that the roles originate from ancient times and, through thousands of years of living close together with kin, have become the nature of the Chinese. Thus to truly understand the youth it is important to look at the types of obligations and relationships in Chinese society that inherently differ from those in the West.

In Chinese society, the roles of husband and wife are clearly defined. The wife's duty is to take care of her husband, children, parents, and household. The wife controls the activities of the household but depends on her husband for economic support. On the other hand, the husband is the king of the household. His major duty is to provide financial support for his parents and his own family, giving money to his wife to spend for the household. He traditionally kept his hands out of domestic chores because he was coddled by his own parents as a child and made dependent on his mother for food and support. He thus does not know how to perform household activities and reasons that he needs a wife to do them. Yet, it is customary for the male to drive the family car, with the female comfortably sitting in the back seat. Should his wife earn more at her occupation, which has happened more frequently in recent years, the husband generally feels humiliated. In any case, husband and wife share the same task of pushing their child to obtain good grades.

In modern times, both male and female children must receive excellent scores on their college entrance exam to gain acceptance to a prestigious university. They must take care of their parents, both physically and economically, and honor relatives and elders. Meanwhile, their mother prepares food and cleans the house for them, although doting grandparents often take care of them while their parents are at work. The presence of grandparents in raising grandchildren can cause conflict between parents and grandparents, each generation spoiling the child in its own way and arguing that its way is the best way to cultivate the child's morals.

Parents most likely will help the child in purchasing a house out of their savings because it is nearly impossible for a young person to do so entirely on his or her own means. In this respect, the child is dependent on the family's assistance for survival. The child will reciprocate by paying for expenses in the parents' old age.

The familial system thus encourages dependence among people and institutions (without the negative American connotations). When that dependency is unfulfilled, people become confused and may ask what went wrong. Every person obeys the government if it respects the person and maintains the social order.[1] Further, everybody respects and follows traditions because ancestors are believed to be closer to heaven and morally superior.[2] It is this system of obligations that ultimately ties the family together and guarantees its continuity.

Obviously, the teenagers give family the highest importance rating, followed by school and friends. Their high rating suggests that they will make sacrifices and care for their parents. Family is also an important factor in socializing, since it is very common in China for teenagers to socialize with parents on the weekends. My home-stay brother was astonished when he heard that Americans do not often "go out" with their parents, brothers, or sisters on a Saturday night. He, along with many other teenagers, has hardly ever "gone out" with friends in his spare time.

In addition to increased interaction, the family unit is strengthened by conservative teachings and traditions. Because people are generally less individualistic, adults in marriage are more resigned to difficult situations than their American counterparts and will try to make the best of them. This acceptance is best illustrated in the instance of an unhappy Chinese wife who, rather than divorce her horrible husband, will keep the family intact and consider the good aspects of her husband—such as his urging her to pursue her goals. The benefits of the cohesive Chinese family, security and attention, keep the youth accepting their familial situations. Gu M. gave great insight into Chinese society by stating that the finest aspect of Chinese society is that everybody fits in and is taken care of.

Throughout Chinese history, bureaucratic officials traditionally had to take numerous rigorous examinations that required strict memorization of Confucian sayings, advocating a moral education that stressed familial cohesion. Those who passed examinations gained higher status and were believed by the emperor to be more loyal and became part of the elite. This tradition has not varied significantly over a couple of millennia because tests are still molded in this fashion, and the sense of history that is part of that tradition gives the system a feeling of naturalness to the Chinese. Confucian values about the family still play a role in hiring employees for jobs in bureaucracy and state-owned companies because some of these institutions look at the prospective employee's family social connections, known as *guanxi*, before hiring.

Clearly binding the Chinese family unit is the one-child policy, which forces parents to hold dear to them the sole individual perpetuating the family line. Parents and grandparents are thus able to overwhelm their single children with attention and material gifts as well as make them fully dependent on the family, thus explaining the teens' relatively immature behaviors. The one-child policy makes the term "little emperor" appropriate in that these single spoiled children live under a 4-2-1 generation tree, with four grandparents and two parents revolving around them. A child is the sole beneficiary of holiday gifts and inheritances from most of these older individuals, who historically have had a high savings rate. Moreover, as a singleton a child is prone to being fed more, explaining the plump physiques of some Chinese teenagers. Although Generation Y teenagers are not solely without the presence of siblings because cousins often take the role of sisters and brothers, they do not have to deal with siblings on a daily basis.

Though the one-child policy allows for the highest allocation of family resources to the development of a single child, it has predisposed the youth to find it difficult to share and socialize with others, resulting in coddled youth. Lauren Buckalew of CBC Research Shanghai explains, "Arguably, China's economic leap since the 1980s has made it possible for average students to make a living, and more after-school activities such as music and art lessons are available where none were before. However, the entrance exam has not gotten any easier, creating a prisoner's dilemma for parents and teachers, who are evaluated on their students' test performance: should they foster a child's personal interests at the risk of a lower score?—not if it gives other classmates an edge. Thus, parents shelter children; activities that detract from study time are not simply discouraged but are bypassed completely. Children are coddled, and parents create a home environment free from distractions that take children's minds off test preparation material. By the time students grow up, personal dreams and aspirations no longer have meaning, having been displaced by a sense of obligation to one's family to attend a prestigious university and make a handsome salary."

Teenagers have a few fears. Yu Q. fears insects, while another male fears his friends backstabbing him. But hardly mentioned were larger concerns that they and their generation may face in the future. Gen Y teens are beginning to see that their parents' policies are causing them problems. Zhang explains Gen Y's low tolerance to emotional shocks:

Zhang: Students now—actually sometimes their ability to endure things mentally is rather poor and very weak. It's easy to take a blow and then immediately not be OK. This kind of situation is very serious among my friends and the people around me.

It seems that the fusion of Chinese culture with modern life has created a void in the lives of the youth. As a result of the tremendous stress from school and parents' strong control in the social lives of their little emperors, teenagers are finding it more difficult to make friends and confide to them their problems. In a survey, the Beijing Working Committee on Women and Children found that students have a rough time dealing with their stress. Generally at the age of 15 (the age at which students take entrance exams and start secondary school), children have fewer friends with whom to talk about their problems.[3] Consequently, China's youth are left alone amidst a mound of problems and a weak support system. Their social skills are affected while their propensity for abusing alcohol and committing crime and suicide increases.

Increased interaction breeds friction between China's Gen Yers and their parents. For instance, dating and family-building are highly regulated by social customs. A person must marry around the age of 25 or at least be on the road to doing so, giving the person about five years to choose the one with whom to spend the rest of his or her life. Any older than this, people will be considered misfits to society and will have greater difficult in finding a spouse. Parental pressure put on Gen Y is heightened as the youth near this age. Parents see this to be the right age to follow tradition, naturally demanding a grandchild on whom they can dote. The parents' values of proper childbearing are inherently contradictory to those brought about by modernization, which advocate childbearing at later ages. Furthermore, a child must adhere to the rules of his or her parents in order to marry a spouse whom their parents approve. Clearly, this can cause problems between the generations and complicate an already complicated system that bans dating until college.

The Generation Gap

Modernization has resulted in a tangible generation gap between Gen Yers and their parents and grandparents. The majority of teens in my study mentioned they were unable to communicate easily with their parents due to discrepancies in values and ideas; the teenagers believe that life is vastly dissimilar for the two generations. Two teenagers explain the gap:

> Zhang: For example, in terms of my friends, my parents think it's OK for us to be friends. I think it's OK too. But they hope that I make friends with people who have better grades than I do, and not to make friends with people who do worse, or with people who like to dress up, since they think that girls who like to look nice don't want to study hard. I think there's a generation gap in this respect.

> A plump teenager mentioned: I go to my room after school. I will only speak to them when I want help. I will avoid talking to them because I think it's a waste of time. There is a deep generation gap between us. Our conceptions are very different. Like clothes, for example: parents cannot accept clothing… They want me to wear leather shoes [at a white-collar job] and I don't want to.

Chinese youth have different outlooks on the future primarily because they are more optimistic than their parents. They exude optimism in their forecasts for the future and their dreams, ultimately affecting their career pursuits and triggering apathy in some teens. In contrast to their parents, Generation Y in Shanghai is overwhelmingly receptive to the tall buildings and development occurring in most large Chinese urban areas, believing that life and living conditions will improve in China for both rural and urban residents.

> Han, 17: I think my parents are not optimistic enough. I can't talk to them.

Further perpetuating the generation divide is the importance of age reverence in traditional Chinese culture. Chinese society requires that one show honor and respect to older kin. Consequently, it is very normal for Chinese youth to be talked down to by parents who are believed to be sager, causing Generation Y to feel supervised and belittled. Ge W. expressed his anger when he learned his mother had snooped in his backpack and investigated his cell phone for any intimation of a girlfriend. Zhang, a female, told a similar story:

> Zhang: Actually, I told my mom that my grades are just so-so now, and if I found a boyfriend maybe my grades would get better. He wouldn't necessarily have a negative effect and could help me with school. My mom only said, "You're so little. What kind of love can you understand?" Geez.

I must admit that I encountered similar treatment from my home-stay parents and numerous other adults, including a police officer in Beijing with whom I came into contact. They treated me as a child in spite of my unchild-like undertaking of writing a book. Although this custom sharply differs from Western individualistic values, I readily accepted this aspect of Chinese culture, just as Gen Y teens do on a daily basis. Indeed, I was honored that my home-stay mother would protect me as if I were her own child.

Last, desires of being independent bolster the generation gap. Because of filial piety beliefs, parents in China heavily influence teenagers' future occupation, their likes and dislikes, spouse, and other aspects of their lives. Teenagers are thus dependent on their parents' and government's decisions and support. However, the advent of modernization and consumerism has naturally caused the youth to experience some forms of independence and feel a greater need to be independent. As the Chinese struggle to choose their economic and political path, the youth will choose their degree of individuality and freedom in societal relationships.

> Tao L.: I personally think, if you can be independent—well, I want to be as independent as possible (and) not to absolutely and completely depend on my parents. After all, once you reach the age when you can be independent, your parents will still have their lives too; if you always depend on them, they will get tired and you won't be able to take care of yourself.

> Zhu: I think it's okay that I can be completely independent and not need to depend on my parents. I hope to own a large house and a car.

Gu Y. analyzes the differences between cultures in the context of individualism:

Do you think that foreigners are too individualistic?

You can say that their individuality breeds more individuality. Chinese people have a group mentality—I'll give an example: Americans like to play Bridge, [which uses] two-on-two, mutual assistance to fight the enemy. Japanese people play Go; they have the spirit of samurai, one-on-one. Chinese people play Mahjong, watching the players on both sides, the Upper House [*ding shang jia*] and the Lower House [*ding xia jia*]. At a certain time—when things are stable, af-

95

ter society is stable—China will want to open up. Why did people used to say that China was a sleeping lion? Because at that time China was so cool; it waited until enemies invaded, then it would all just explode.

The frequent and pervasive complaints voiced by teenagers indicate the existence of a much larger generation gap between China's Gen Y and its parents than exists in the United States. Although American teenagers and their parents may disagree on the grounds they have nothing in common with each other, American parents generally understand the phases of adolescence and the effects of modernization, and often grant teenagers freedom to be teenagers. American sitcoms demonstrate this norm: the parents expect teenage behavior and teach their teenager a lesson through adolescent mistakes. Moreover, American parents and teens would probably conclude that a generation gap is to be expected in any and every culture. It might be fair to say that American parents, because of their modern working environment, have a firmer understanding of the lives and desires of the millennial generation than do most Chinese parents.

The generation gap in China seems to be considerably greater than that in the U.S. Every day Chinese youth are adapting at warp speed to new technologies, experiencing even greater change than their American counterparts, while their parents, many of whom work in factories, lack basic computer and Internet literacy. Chinese youth have to mend the gap between their generation and their sentimentally close, yet very traditional, parents, most of whom are still in the dark about consumerism and capitalism. They also have to find, in their own way, a mean between traditional and Western beliefs, which in many cases are contradictory.

On the other hand, Chinese parents also have different perspectives. Their struggles in earlier times were more somber. In their day a college education was exceedingly difficult to attain because the nation lacked resources to educate the populace. During the Cultural Revolution, many educated people were either killed or ordered to go to labor camps in the countryside. Many parents of Gen Y teens grew up in poverty, usually working in the fields or factories. The major concern on their minds involved their next meal, not purchasing a trendy Japanese mobile phone. Because of the tremendous chaos in their country and lives, many parents remained pessimistic throughout their lives. Conversely, Generation Y teens in the prosperous cities of China have significantly fewer worries. Contrary to the opinions of their parents, many teens believe that there is more to life than toiling at school just to make more money in the long run; they want to "have a life." Teenagers even wish to pursue singing and careers in graphic design or as a DJ. The difference in values not only makes some teens feel truly uneasy at home, but also encourages the youth to keep secrets from their parents, only discussing school matters with them. Teenagers are increasingly turning to friends and others to fill the communication void. One female mentioned that she spends at least an hour a day conversing with friends. In addition, the popularity of the Internet is causing many Gen Yers to turn to Internet buddies in chat rooms for advice.

With the spoiling of single children, consistent interaction with demanding parents, and a noticeable generation gap, a rise in rebellion is expected. "I do not want to be restrained by anyone," says one teenager. "I want to do whatever I want to do," says another. "I will be free when parents are not home," says a male. Even older females, who have much closer relationships with their families, realize the huge differences with their parents. "We have different thinking," says an older female. Another responds, "We [as a generation] are more open." "We have different values and morals in life. They [American teenagers] feel a lot of love in America... Here you don't think about anything; everything is prepared for you. Chinese parents treat you like children."

Rebellion is especially palpable among the oldest boys who do not listen to their parents. Parents have ambitions for their sons to become doctors and other high positions to make a lot of money, but some of the older boys do not necessarily want to "wear loafers" when they grow up, preferring to relax, date, and play computer games. The most they interact with their parents is during family visits to the home of their grandparents, and they keep most of their personal affairs private, especially their dating and cell phone charges. Ge W. is indignant at his mother's surreptitious snooping in his backpack. Like a scavenger, he says, she reads the text messages on his cell phone, hunting for any trace of a girlfriend. He desires to rent an apartment near his school to escape the often unfounded accusations of his mother and to fulfill his dream to be free. His new life would be an experiment that is unlikely to occur. He escapes these troubles by going to the local Internet café with his friends.

Customs are changing so quickly that dating is no longer taboo for the youth, an idea that makes grandparents, and even parents, shudder. Parents make it clear that dating is forbidden, and yet the youth disobey such commands. A few teenagers admitted to lying to their parents to obtain more personal freedom. The youth are choosing their own path in this regard, essentially rebelling against the prohibition of dating:

What do you think about dating, dating between girls and boys?

Qin: It's quite normal.

But your teachers and the school seem not to agree with such behavior, do they?

Qin: We do such things secretly.

Some older Gen Yers who decided to divorce their spouses rebelled against traditional society and the wills of their parents. In 2003, nearly 1.33 million couples in China dissolved their marriages—154,000 more than in the previous year. One teen in a technical school estimated that one-fifth of her classmates have broken families. Many conservatives blame this rise in divorce on Western influences, increased female economic power, and relaxed restrictions on divorce since 2001.[4] The popularity of divorce and its glamorization are illustrated by the impressive ratings and sold-out status of the soap opera *Divorce Chinese Style*. When a couple decides to get divorced, the husband, because of his economic power and traditional Chinese values that stress the importance of perpetuating the family name, sometimes gains custody over the couple's child. The wife can even be left homeless if her husband's company owns the couple's apartment. Although many spouses are throwing in the towel, a far greater number of husbands and wives remain in their marriages to prevent gossip, familial backlashes, incessant paperwork, and breaches of traditional values.

On the streets in Hong Kong and Shanghai it is evident that China's youth are rebelling against traditional culture. This generation is set apart by its adoption of hair dye, trendy clothing, music, tattoos, piercings, makeup, and new technological toys, often used to escape interaction with parents. Teenagers follow such practices to be trendy and also to express their frustrations with society. Both are equally prevalent, though the former is more easily admitted.

Have you ever felt that people the same age as you…there would be one person who was dissatisfied with society?

We all are.

Someone who felt really angry?

There's no anger, but there is a sense of helplessness. There's nothing we can do about this society. This society had problems from the beginning.

99

Do you choose to remain silent about your dissatisfaction, or do you use your words and actions to express it?

Well…it's just…like people who like to dance, they dance. It is a way of expressing themselves.

You can use music to release your feelings?

Music has no borders.

—Gu Y.

Although Chinese youth's demeanor is rebelling against traditional society and its restriction of personal freedom, we must be wary about the extent of the breakdown, because teenagers by and large still follow Confucian ideals of obedience and filial piety. Not all respondents vehemently rebuked societal constraints and lack of freedom. Many of the girls plan to fulfill their obligations of filial piety by buying their parents big houses. Older girls seem to have the deepest connection with their parents, as they will shop, surf the Internet, and sing with their parents. Zhang even drinks with her father to open up to him and build up a tolerance for alcohol at social events where it is customary to drink. Though some Chinese youth have ideas about freedom, none would want to see parents living in a nursing home, which has emerged in China only recently. The youth in all probability will become more independent but will not relinquish their filial roles, essentially creating a watered-down version of today's strict relationship obligations.

Male and Female Relations

In the past, Chinese society, like that of Japan, favored the male sex over the female. This bias is evident through China's staggering disparity between births of females and males: approximately 106 males per every 100 females.[5] Favoritism of the sexes has existed in the past because of the agrarian lifestyle that required many men to do hard labor in the fields and women to do work inside the home. Though times have changed, the stigmas and taboos on female and male behavior are still palpable. For example, it is proper for a Chinese male to drink beer and smoke but not for a female. In addition, my host family's wife was not allowed to drive the family car around Shanghai, though she mentioned she did not want to. Gen Y teenagers have different values in that more females want to participate in many of the male-dominated activities, such as driving cars, drinking, and purchasing homes.

The gender roles are undergoing rapid change with the massive socio-economic changes that grip the Middle Kingdom. More and more, women are rapidly climbing the social ladder and earning more money, and the future of gender roles is becoming less predictable. The older females are divided in their prediction of the changing household roles of men and women, with half believing the sexes will become more equal and the other half contending that the roles will remain the same. "China is traditional," one said, and was reticent in wanting any change. However, they believe that women will be more equal at least in their careers and will bring their own wealth to the table in the future. If a greater number of women earn more than their husbands and remain in their careers after childbirth, not only would the marketplace and the nation's growth rate change, but also would societal norms.

Males and females have definite ideas on the opposite sex. Males see themselves as different from females, whom they view as particularistic—mostly focused on smaller issues—potentially adding to culturally perceived differences between genders. Both sexes accept the bias that men are stronger in mathematics and sciences. However, the sexes differ in their descriptions of each other's general behavior. One female called males "arrogant," whereupon a male retorted, "Girls are sensitive. They like dreaming and fantasy." Another male followed, "Girls are easily angered." Teenagers accept that females studied harder and are overprotected by their parents, while males spent more time having fun and playing on computers. These strong beliefs about gender result from the limited contact between males and females during their adolescence.

Societal Differences

In China, have you ever felt that everyone places high importance on family?

Confucian education.

Why do you think that this has come about? You mentioned Confucian education. After all these years, is it Confucianism or are there other elements to education?

"Above all, respect for your elders" [Confucian quote]. A lot of these appeared out of folk culture. There is a very deep history there, reflecting the way society is. You can see each development in some other countries. They say that Japan's aim is to take things from other cultures, then make more of them. China is one way, the U.S. is another way; each country has its unique points. The German people place importance on precision, so German people's work is so very good; they make precision machinery. The Japanese machine industry is bad, but they make good electronics. They take electronics that Americans have invented, and make them like this—no one had ever thought of that.

—Gu Y.

Guanxi is an important concept in Chinese culture to which Gen Y adheres, for it plays a key role in business, consumption, leisure, and even politics. *Guanxi* is a network of connections and relationships that help a person obtain items above and beyond what the masses can. Wealth, skill, reputation, and family status all determine one's *guanxi*. In the past, having high-powered *guanxi* helped people skip the rationing line. In this respect, *guanxi* puts a damper on China's ability to be egalitarian. Business ventures are often established between members of one's *guanxi* because members are close, trustful friends, an important virtue in Chinese culture.[6] Doing business in China requires that a businessman get to know his prospective partner and emotionally trust him, instead of garnering trust by means of Western contractual obligations.[7] *Guanxi* corruption is also evident throughout China, manifesting itself in the form of people pulling strings to pay cheaper prices for goods and services. For instance, in Shanghai party officials with these contacts could have priority over others in finding office space. *Guanxi* played an important role in state corporations hiring young college students because family status and connections were partially used as a barometer to evaluate an employee's aptitude.[8] Rural residents use *guanxi* to access better doctors, among many other privileges.

So you want to start your partnership in Shanghai. Have you thought of going anywhere else?

I don't have friends anywhere else. I wouldn't leave.

"Losing face," or losing respect in another person's eyes, is an important way to lose *guanxi*. The Chinese as well as people in many other Asian cultures do not take well to others screaming at them, because that in turn causes them to lose face. Often, a person being yelled at will smile in spite of his or her anger in order to "save face" in front of others. Gaining face, or building one's status, is important in building a *guanxi* network, and is done by gaining respect and having others indebted to you.

Notes

[1]http://www.empereur.com/DOC/Confucian_political_theory.html.

[2]http://www.wsu.edu:8080/~dee/CHPHIL/CONF.HTM.

[3]http://china.org.cn/english/2003/Jul/69842.htm.

[4]http://www.china.org.cn/english/Life/95643.htm.

[5]CIA World Factbook. Last updated June 30, 2005.

[6]*Global Gold* by Ruth Stanat.

[7]http://chinese-school.netfirms.com/goldenhints.html.

[8]*China Urban* by Suzanne Gottschang and Lyn Jeffery. "Guiding College Graduates to Work" in Dalian, p. 65.

Chapter 5

Living Environment

Many in the developed world have inaccurate preconceptions about the housing and living conditions in China. Most Americans who have never ventured to the country would presume that a billion Chinese are starving and walking barefoot on the streets. They would probably be oblivious to the traditions and meanings that are present in the lives of 1.3 billion people, including Generation Y.

The youth are beset in a world of different living conditions. They live in different homes, eat different foods, and deal with different problems. However, modernization is bringing the Chinese youth closer to the developed world, increasingly predisposing them to the same situations and problems as Westerners. Their living arrangements and the traditions they follow form the basis of their behavior. How can America work together with the Chinese youth in the global market without knowing such a powerful and large group of people? We must walk, or perhaps bike, a mile in the youth's shoes to understand their thoughts and lifestyles.

Housing

The Western preconception of small houses in China is accurate. As a result of the government's regulation over family size, apartments are specifically made for three persons. In many cases residences only contain one bedroom for the family: mother, father, and child. It is not unusual to have extended family members living and sleeping in the same quarters in a home. One teen mentioned that she sleeps in her mother's bedroom. As people become wealthier, they may purchase adjoining studio apartments for their younger child or their parents. My home-stay family had an apartment for its grandparents, an adjoining studio apartment for me (normally inhabited by Tim, my home-stay brother), a kitchen, a bathroom, a small living room, a small bedroom for the son, and a small bedroom for the parents. Governmentally mandated housing arrangements allow the government to assert itself into the populace's daily lives and to make families become more cohesive units. Close living quarters work in China because of Confucian values of filial piety.

Certainly the urban landscape differs from the rural landscape. Similar to many other Asian cities, Chinese cities are vertical and clustered together and quickly becoming more so. Elevators are a luxury, but are becoming more commonplace as walls and walls of skyscraper residential buildings Westernize. Apartment buildings increasingly are becoming larger and more closely modeled on Western architecture. In Shanghai, some buildings now so closely resemble those in Miami or New York that it is easy to forget where they are. Because of severe pollution and rust, common colors of the exteriors of apartment buildings are brown and gray, changing different hues within a few years after buildings are completed. Small capitalists have begun to invest in property ever since the government relaxed the housing market, allowing the market to define housing prices for its citizens. Shanghai is currently believed to be one of the three biggest real estate boomtowns in the world with the top emerging real estate markets of which to take advantage.

In contrast, housing in rural areas is starkly different. In the vast rural areas, houses are even smaller and vary by region; they are often of poor quality and sometimes cause health hazards to the inhabitants. One significant problem with Chinese construction is that the builder will subcontract to another subcontractor, who will, in turn, subcontract to still another. The final re-

My bedroom, originally that of my home-stay brother Tim, at the Zheng apartment in Puxi, Shanghai.

Tim, Ben (a friend of Tim's), and I pose after a game of tennis in Ben's affluent subdivision in Shanghai.

The Zhengs pose in front of shops in Yuyuan Gardens in Shanghai, a scene that illuminates China's capitalist energy.

A television host delivers entertainment and music news to Chinese teenagers.

Chinese teenagers watch their favorite stars perform on a pop culture channel on television.

Two Gen Y girls exemplify the spirit of their generation.

A typical class-room at a high school in Shanghai.

School in China: The domain in which Gen Y teenagers slave during their adolescence.

Living in the 19th century house but dressed in the 21st century clothes: A Gen Y girl walks home from school in her Beijing *Hutong* (antique residential alleyways).

Photos on this page show teenagers in Shanghai

Comic books are getting popular among teenage boys and girls.

Right:
Singing karaoke.

Bottom left:
At an Internet café.

Bottom right:
At the sports section of a department store.

The house of a prominent, affluent business colleague of the Zhengs in a luxurious Western-style subdivision on the outskirts of Shanghai

An affluent Shanghai suburb where a business colleague of the Zhengs lived.

An old residential area in Beijing.

A typical hallway in an urban lower-middle class apartment building in Shanghai.

An exposition that shows Shanghai's plans for the future.

Highrises under construction in Shanghai and a sign that says "Do Not Spit," which shows how the Chinese care about hygiene.

Building China: Millions of migrant workers from rural areas flock to cities like Shanghai to build skyscrapers and public works.

People gaze at the stores, advertisements, and new constructions on Nanjing West Road, one of the most popular walking paths in central Shanghai.

Chinese teenagers know more about McDonald's than any other Western food.

The Kernel is a common meeting ground for Gen Y teens.

The City of Lights: Shanghai's Nanjing Road more closely resembles Las Vegas with its lights and neon signs than the Chinese financial capital.

Tiananmen Square: An emblem of Chinese communism and the site of the 1989 democracy demonstrations.

Two lions guarding the Emperor's Palace in Beijing.

On top of a great dragon, I stand on the Great Wall, a vestige of the Middle Kingdom's ancient past.

sult is a toxic paint imported for the countryside, where health is not of significant importance. The same noxious paint is present in some of the large, well-known luxury hotels in Shanghai. Furthermore, the structures of the houses are sometimes unstable because poor materials are used for their construction. One suburban village of mansions built for expatriates was so poorly constructed that the houses now need renovation only a few years later. Generation Y is more receptive to the new Western-style apartment buildings arriving in Shanghai. One female yearns for a home made from a foreign country because she is tired of Chinese-style housing. On the same note, she continued that Chinese houses "are not free."

The youth, however, yearn for Western-made houses and are familiar with the expatriate living quarters in Shanghai, which look more or less like Italian architecture villas placed closely together in a neat American subdivision. The Chinese constitution was recently modified so that it now guarantees the right to private property. It allows foreigners to purchase the property, already expensive because of real estate bubbles in large cities, and hold it for 70 years. After that, nobody knows what will happen. Actually, nobody can predict what can happen because there is no guarantee that the legal system will protect land rights or that the government won't repudiate property laws and confiscate the land.

The exterior of many residences in China may be considered decrepit by Western standards. Some streets in Chinese cities resemble those in downtown Beirut with building debris and rubbish scattered carelessly about. The reason for such superficially unattractive exteriors is because the Chinese are generally more concerned with the inside of their houses, which are kept clean by either a mother or an *Ayi* (a maid)—unlike the United States, which is obsessed with home improvement. This is best illustrated by the exteriors of the rows and rows of apartment buildings speckled with colorful articles of laundry set out to dry. Further, Westerners may be initially surprised if invited as guests to visit friends' houses, because they will be required to replace their shoes for sandals for purposes of cleanliness. Walking on floors without sandals would procure the same reaction as sticking one's hand in a bowl of food in the West. Many people in Hong Kong and Southern China follow the teachings of Feng Shui, an ancient Chinese practice of harnessing energy through the location of objects and buildings. In Shanghai and other Chinese cities, many families place red scrolls with gold lettering on their walls for good luck.

Beijing is renowned for its *hutong* or alleyways, which are only 30 feet wide from building to building. These old tenements are believed to be a historical remnant of Chinese culture and history and soon to be an endangered piece of the past. Modern buildings and infrastructure clash with the old, historic courtyards of the *hutong*. The government gladly offers residents modern homes outside of the *hutong*, and many individuals have gladly relocated and embraced a more modern life. Yet some residents continue to reside in the decrepit alleys. Why would a family still want to live in the same ostensibly dilapidated shack with other families, sharing rooms and toilets, despite offers of new, modern housing? First, many remain there because of the *hutong's* sense of community. Nonfamily residents provide security and friendship and can also perform chores for a family. Descriptions of life exist in the "we" form instead of the "I," unlike in America. Also, the *hutong* exudes a sense of crucial history to the Beijingese, and some residents do not have the will to move to modern apartments because their kin have lived in *hutong* for generations. Clearly, these important communal values carry great weight in people's lives.

China's Gen Yers are overwhelmingly interested in cleanliness and propriety; they reject the negative rural habits of their parents. For instance, one female responded that she tries to prevent her father from spitting. China is notorious for its spitting, a habit more common in the rural areas of China but still highly present in urban areas. Teens and parents alike are lured to fast-food restaurants not only because of their relaxed atmosphere and food, but also because of their ostensibly sanitary conditions, which are hammered into the minds of the youth when a worker is conspicuously mopping or wiping the restaurant's floors.[1]

The government is taking more steps to regulate housing. In large cities the government is attempting to limit the practice of setting out laundry to dry outside the window. Also, the government is allegedly attempting to clean up the heaps of rubble and litter in many of the large cities like Shanghai in order to attract more expatriates. On a more serious note, the government is evicting residents to allow land developers to destroy dilapidated apartment buildings and build towering, modern apartment buildings. The government will evict a family that has lived in the same building for generations with only three months' notice. Unlike in Western countries, residents in China do not own the land. People rent the land from the government for a period of 70 years and have little recourse in the government's arbitration. The government does offer approximately $12,000 to purchase another residence; however, many families believe that the government's offer is insufficient, for Shanghai is experiencing an unprecedented housing boom, and residents would be forced to move to a distant suburb or rural town.

On a more personal note, Jimmy, a friend of mine, has been told to move in order to build a shopping mall. His family has lived in the same location for countless years; and like others facing the same situation, he is protesting the land grabs. People are beginning to believe that the government is corrupt and is accepting money from developers to destroy old residences. The people may not be too far off: nearly 160,000 cases of evictions were flawed in 2003.[2] Residents have attempted suicide in protestation of the land grabs, as the money offered is insufficient and will cause more financial distress. Wenzhou Hou in the *San Francisco Gate* expressed the people's anger by stating: "There is a growing anger in China that our revolution, which was sup-

109

posed to take property from the rich and give it to the poor, is now taking property from the poor and giving it to the rich." However, one person who attempted suicide and failed now faces two years in prison and torment by police. The judicial system offers no help as courts and lawyers are sternly advised by the government not to take the people's cases for land grabbing and other people's rights cases. This practice, done for the modernization of major cities of China, has caused and will cause many of China's youth like Jimmy to become disheartened with the government's actions.

Not only does housing formulate the behaviors of the youth, but it also results in their freedom as the government asserts its claims in private life. New residences and customs and altered relationships that result are all changes affecting the youth and changing their mind-sets, either positively or negatively.

Food and Customs

Also coming to the Chinese Mainland are American Ambassadors Colonel Sanders and Ronald McDonald, who have made their marks on Generation Y. In just two decades these Western food chains have started from one restaurant and expanded to hundreds of restaurants nationwide, making the dining experience not so much based on the quality of the food as on the exotic, relaxed atmosphere that caters to young, modern teens. But the new Western foods introduced to China have more significance than at first glance. Obviously, the new fast foods from the West differ sharply in composition from the foods from the East. However, food in China is more than just something with which to fill a stomach; it carries with it important connotations and meanings, which are especially held dear by Gen Yers' parents. Western foods and their marketing have been interfering with transmission of traditional eating habits to Gen Y. Traditionally, older generations adhere to ideas about balancing *yin* and *yang* of Taoist philosophy in regard to food and follow the belief by eating opposite food types, such as hot and cold foods.[3] It is of interest to note that along with economic reforms, consumption of different food types has changed dramatically with a decrease in grains and plants to a drastic increase in meat, chicken, eggs, and seafood; the increase is even greater in rural areas from 1981-1987.

Gen Y in urban areas has less propensity to follow these traditional ideas than its rural compatriots because of their proximity to fast-food restaurants and Western marketing. For instance, Gen Y teens in Shanghai who have watched television and walked by fast-food restaurants are much more likely to coerce their wealthier parents to feed them Western food, especially before and after important school events. They also hear more about KFC and McDonald's from their friends at school; consequently, the youth yearn for such food even if they have not tasted it. The success of Western food chains can also be attributed to the growth in the number of affluent families, the corporations' techniques in targeting the children, and especially the rise of youth purchasing power due to the change in living conditions and parental doting caused by the one-child policy. In addition, fast-food restaurants have become part of the diets of many Chinese because the restaurants have successfully assimilated to local social life in addition to local food tastes. KFC, among the most popular fast-food chains in the country, equips some of its restaurants with playpens and new drive-up windows to accommodate wealthy families, whose children further add to the hype by sharing their experiences and toys from these restaurants at the school lunch table. To entice energetic children, many KFC restaurants have shorter seats to accommodate the young and have decorated their walls with cartoons, especially murals of Qiki (Chicky), the cartoon of the young Colonel Sanders made specifically for young people. The chain capitalizes on childhood birthday parties, at which some parents will spend more than 1,000 RMB ($125), and has made eating at KFC an important part of the celebration. For instance,

Jiang Q. finds the best gift he could give someone was a Western-style birthday cake, in contrast with the traditional eggs and long stranded noodles, signifying longevity, usually given during the birthday. Other domestic fast-food restaurants, such as Zheng Guang He and Yong He Dou Jiang, copy these techniques and emphasize their Chinese food with a Western atmosphere. The new fast-food companies instill in Gen Y an important value—consumer choice, which is making China even more capitalistic.[4]

Despite the fact that about half of the youth love fast food, the Chinese in general love their nation's food and in actuality know very little about foreign foods because of the dearth of foreign restaurants. Most of the foreign restaurants in China serve either Japanese or Cantonese and other provincial foods. As a result, my host family had no idea that Western food is different from Chinese food. They were astounded to hear that Americans do not eat soup and dumplings for breakfast. Most kitchens are not equipped with ovens to cook Western meals. Usually, wealthy business executives are the only patrons of Western food due to the price and the perceived sophistication of the food. Because the Chinese do not eat Western food, it should also come as no surprise that most are unable to use forks and spoons.

Chinese food is completely different from Western food and quite different from that of American Chinese restaurants. Unlike in America, restaurants often serve meals with a rotating glass plate with platters of different foods. Diners at restaurants will get their food by rotating the center plate and serving themselves from the dishes. At home, a family will often place the plates in the center of the table.

Unlike in the United States, the Chinese do not separate breakfast foods from the foods of other meals. Thus breakfast can consist of soups, noodles, rice and/or dumplings. Lunch usually consists of noodle soups, dumplings, or rice with meat dishes. Dinner typically consists of a wider variety of food such

112

as fish, vegetables, chicken, beef, and soup. The food from the plates is often placed on top of the sticky, white rice in front of the eater. Chopsticks are the only utensils used for eating; large soup spoons are sometimes used to dish food out of the communal bowls. Chinese cuisine serves soups at every meal of the day. Traditionally, people do not drink Coke (or *kele* as it is pronounced in Chinese) with their meals; they drink the broth of the soup for refreshment. Almost every Chinese home and restaurant serves food containing monosodium glutamate—a salt from seaweed that looks similar to table salt—that makes the eater feel good and want to eat more. Many believe that the substance is addictive; it has been known to cause serious health problems, such as allergic reactions and heart problems.

The Chinese generally do not have the table manners that Westerners would consider proper. Diners often make loud slurping noises to gobble the tiny pieces of rice in their bowls. Many people also chew and speak with their mouths open. Moreover, in many restaurants it is expected to lay chicken bones on the table; at other times one places bones and seeds in a separate bowl. Hosts will keep refilling your plate as soon as you finish eating. Additionally, it is also tolerable in Chinese cuisine for someone to reach and grab food before somebody else takes it.

Food, with all of its symbolism and meaning, plays an important role in Chinese holidays. The most important of them, the Chinese New Year, brings the family together around the table. Traditionally, the Chinese have 10-12-plate feasts, for even numbers predict double the amount of good luck. These societal relations are as important as ever during holidays, when family members congregate to celebrate traditions such as the Chinese New Year, the Dragon Boat Festival, the Lantern Festival, the Mid-Autumn Festival, and the Winter Festival. Children are taught about the correct food types for specific moods and holidays. For the Dragon Boat Festival, people will eat *zongzi*, a ball of rice filled with nuts, vegetables, and fruits and wrapped in bamboo leaves. During the Lantern Festival, which marks the end of the lunar year celebrations, families will eat sweet dumplings, or *yuan xiao*. At the Mid-Autumn Festival families will eat moon cakes shaped to celebrate the visibly larger moon during that time of the lunar month. Families will usually eat porridges of nuts, seeds, and vegetables during the Winter Festival. However, some believe the *little emperors* are not receiving the transmission of these crucial elements of tradition. Children in Jiangsu province knew when to eat certain dishes but did not know the significance of every dish, in contrast to their grandparents.[5] Western food symbolism of fun and excitement contrasts with the significant food symbolism of luck, longevity, and respect, among other connotations.

The seemingly abundant amount and stimulating nature of the food available to Gen Y youth sharply differ from the not-so-rosy picture fifty or even twenty years ago. Their grandparents and parents lived and suffered under the three-year famine (1959-61), the most devastating famine in human history that killed 30 million people,[6] caused by the failure of Mao Zedong's Great Leap Forward.[7] During the three years of famine, nearly 90 million children were born, becoming a huge contingent of Gen Y's parents.

Of course, with the introduction of new and visually stimulating fast foods comes the fattening-up of a generation. The ever-increasing presence of Western fast-food restaurants is creating an epidemic that China has rarely known before—obesity. Along with the increase of their salaries, people have become extravagant with their eating habits, treating themselves to the newly arrived KFC and McDonald's. Nearly one in ten middle schoolers in Shanghai is obese and the national percentage of urban obesity is around eight percent of the youth population.[8] A recent article claimed that "for China, the emergence of a weight problem represents a change without precedent in the country's modern history. Dietary and lifestyle changes that emerged in the United States over several generations of industrialization have swept urban China in just one."[9]

Fueling the change to different, even harmful, eating habits is the rise in purchasing power amongst Gen Y teenagers, which has given the youth an outlet to disobey their parents' decrees about which food they can purchase and eat. Zhang (F, 17) disobeyed her father's orders forbidding her to purchase Ajisen Noodles costing 10-20 RMB, and she did it anyway, eating them in secret. Also, with new television advertising, a high propensity to follow new trends, and no legal drinking age, alcohol is easily becoming more accessible, surging into major alcoholism. Gen Y, mostly individuals nearing graduation and university entrance, finds alcohol at the emerging nightclubs and karaoke bars.

More holidays are being added to the urban youths' calendars like Christmas, Halloween, Mother's Day and Father's Day.[10] Christmas is a popular fad hitting mostly Hong Kong, but slowly permeating Shanghai and other large cities. Some younger parents and children are enamored by the consumerist and decorative nature of the holiday and its tendency to bring family together, rather than by its spiritual aspect. Many stores, including Carrefour Hypermarket, are even decorated with well-known images of the white-haired Santa during the season to lure in children.[11] Decorations for Western-style weddings, such as the white gown and red carpet, are becoming more popular among the youth. These weddings differ from the traditional customs of chanting toasts to each spouse and paying respect to the earth's elements, and even from weddings during the 1970s, when the newlyweds would pose in front of an image of Chairman Mao and recite the sayings of communist thinkers.[12] Part of the allure to young children is the excitement and romanticism created by the holidays. Aiding the spread of all of these fads are Western marketers, movies, and local entrepreneurs who capitalize on this fever. Their use of the holidays is not an indication of their conversion to Western ideas, but the result of a yearning to add new elements to holidays that are complementary to consumer culture.

Transportation

Transportation is a daily concern for Generation Y. The most popular modes of transportation in Shanghai are bikes, taxis, buses, and subways. Biking is the most popular way for transportation because nearly 500 million people including teenagers have possession of a bike.[13] It often feels as though all 500 million bicycles were in Shanghai, since there are so many on the streets. The teens bike for approximately 10-30 minutes each way to go to school. Biking is an efficient way to escape car traffic and to gain exercise during a stage in teenagers' lives when free time is extremely limited. Bicycling does have its dangers in large cities, as the streets in Shanghai sometimes are chaotic. Biking can be especially dangerous during rush hours when the sheer number of bikes can barely fit into the specified lanes. Bikers also have to deal with aggressive drivers, especially those who drive into biker lanes to cut ahead of a traffic jam.

Cars are now the rage in China and the dream of Chinese youth. During the past several years, car manufacturers have been inundating the booming Chinese market. In the Beijing car market, for instance, one in four persons has a car, accounting for nearly two million cars on city roads.[14] In Shanghai, nearly a million and a half vehicles crowd the streets, a figure that will increase by 70,000 cars per year.[15] Volkswagen penetrated the Chinese market twenty years ago and is still the market leader. Foreign car manufacturers can often make larger profits by selling a vehicle in China for the standard price of 40,000 RMB ($5,000) than in a developed nation. BMW, GM, Ford, and Toyota have also been in China for several years. Recently, high-end vehicles such as Ferrari, Bentley, Aston Martin, and Mercedes-Benz's Maybach have entered the Chinese market and plan to steadily sell their vehicles to the nation's elite. China is in the position of

116

America during the 1950s, when everybody had to have a car despite the environmental concerns. In several years China will become the largest car market, surpassing that of the United States and Japan, as even the government is encouraging people to purchase cars in hopes of furthering economic growth.

Of course auto insurance is now becoming more relevant as more and more drivers hit the road. Because the government has deregulated much of the industry because of WTO membership stipulations, foreign and domestic firms have been competing for a stake in the lucrative market. China's Gen Y will be the first generation to truly purchase and sell automobile insurance and life insurance, another indication of China's achievement in becoming a modern nation.

Western-influenced media outlets that had previously gone by the wayside are now beginning to take shape in China. Drive-in theaters have become the newest craze, most notably after dinner hours in Beijing. The emergence and apparent growth in drive-in theaters is due to the fact that many more urban-area families in China have their own cars—another way that current Chinese social changes are parallel to those of the United States during the post World War II era.

The success of the car market has negative implications for China's streets. Many drivers in China are inexperienced, since cars in the past were held only by government officials and a few wealthy people. Now cars are available to a burgeoning middle class that wishes to show off its wealth with fancy toys. Pollution obviously will significantly worsen, giving Gen Y a major environmental quandary to deal with in the future. However, on a smaller level, traffic jams that are now terrible will become unbearable as these toys become commonplace. Not only must Gen Y worry about traffic jams, but the dangers of an untamed driving situation as well. Driving in China is wild; it makes New Jersey drivers look like professionals. Drivers will do almost anything to cut off another vehicle to save several seconds. As a result, when driving in China it may seem that an accident will

117

occur at every second. Fortunately, unlike those in the West, drivers in China have great reflexes in the face of impending danger.

Driving in large cities works in a cycle. Every car switches lanes as soon as the car in front of it lags somewhat behind cars in the lane beside it. As the car attempts to switch lanes, the car behind it in the desired lane will honk incessantly and vigorously attempt to block the neighboring car's cut-off attempt. After many cars in the desired lane overtake the struggling car, it will finally find a pocket to merge. After the car does merge, the car will want to switch lanes again, thus restarting the cycle. Large vehicles such as public buses and transport vehicles excitedly follow the same cycle. Since driving is now open to the general public, accidents in this chaotic system are bound to occur. Driving through the countryside, I witnessed a horrendous accident in which a truck jackknifed, killing several people.

The Chinese driving system itself is illogical, again illustrating China's lack of logistics. A sign of a green illuminated person indicates that it is safe for pedestrians to cross the street, except for the fact that cars are allowed to proceed toward pedestrians because drivers do not follow the equivalent of "No turn on red" signs. Consequently, many pedestrians die as a result of the Chinese driving system. The government has refused to accept the driving systems of other countries that have coherent, time-tested driving experience.

In Shanghai, Beijing, Tianjin, and Guangzhou the government has created or enhanced large subway projects. Shanghai is rapidly expanding its subways system to make the city more like Singapore and other international cities. Migrant construction workers conspicuously work day and night, seven days per week, to construct 715 kilometers of rail in the Shanghai subway. In two decades, subway travel may become the most popular method of transportation in large cities for today's Generation Y.

China's modernization has brought massive pollution to the Middle Kingdom; more people live in noxious pollution in China than in any other country. Children's mental development is affected by pollution right from birth, as infants have been known to have blood-lead levels 80 percent higher than the "dangerous level."[16] Should the government decide to limit pollution, the economy would suffer an economic slowdown, impeding the growth of the country. Government officials' course of action is to allow China to develop first before worrying about pollution, reasoning that the environmental damages can be cleaned up once China becomes a more modern power.

Gen Y is concerned about the environment, specifically the effects of pollution due to rapid industrialization. Most responses were analogous to one teenager's comment: "The environment is very important. It influences people's health and mood." Another older male considered that if the living environment worsened, his and everybody else's lifestyles would suffer.

When more cars replace bicycles on the streets in China and pollution worsens, teenagers and parents will escape to other less polluted cities, making for a more mobile economy. Already the growing middle class can drive to outlying areas and smaller cities on weekends to escape their crowded cities. Soon more families will go to newly built beaches during their newly granted vacations.

Generation Y teens blame the current rise of oil prices on America's war in Iraq. None, however, mentioned that surging oil prices are largely a result of swelling demand from the Chinese economy. Some Gen Yers were somewhat certain that oil prices would affect industrialization in China. Others had no idea about the situation, thus reinforcing the contention that the youth do not often keep abreast of current events or contemplate world issues.

Ethnic Minorities and "Foreigners"

Inherent to a modern economy is not only the flow of information, but also that of people. China is a vast country containing
a wealth of land, people, and ethnicities. It is little wonder that
the third largest—and the most populous—nation in the world
would have nearly 56 different ethnic groups. The major one in
China is the Han, which composes approximately 92 percent of
the Chinese people. Large minorities include the Zhuang,
Manchu, Hui, Miao, and Uighur. Groups such as the Uighurs
occasionally face prejudices as being dirty and barbaric. Chinese teenagers in the large urban areas do not often have to associate with many diverse people, thus potentially adding to the
prevailing prejudices.

Politically, the ethnic groups have been a struggle for the
government, which argues that some minorities and their traditional cultures work against the unification of the country. The
Chinese government has sometimes portrayed its minorities as
exotic and even silly in the media, many times creating rifts between Han and the minority groups. When I asked a teenager
whether he ever wanted to go to Mongolia on an exotic vacation, he declined because "there are not many Han people there."
The government seeks to curtail any potential dissidence by keeping a large police presence in minority areas and ensuring that
minorities study Mandarin. Travelers to Western regions and
Tibet are not allowed to take pictures of sensitive areas or speak
about anything political while there. Recently the government
has used September 11 as an excuse to repress minorities, especially the Muslim Uighurs in the West.

Though the Shanghai teens mentioned that the Chinese are
neutral to all people throughout the world, the youth appear to
be more accepting of foreigners from abroad than of their own
ethnic countrymen in the West of China. Shanghai is historically
reputed to be an international city, where nearly 300,000 expatriates from abroad reside. However, even on tourist streets,

people will sometimes pause, point, or even touch a *waiguoren* (foreigner). Speaking personally, even in the international airport in Guangzhou, China's third largest city, people photographed and videotaped me. Usually, the more rural the town, the more prevalent the staring is.

There has been some perception (or misperception, for that matter) that the Chinese are somewhat racist toward American black people. Almost all the youth, with one exception, said that they accept them, even though they look different. The one exception mentioned he believed black people "look funny," believing that he "[is] superior to them." Several believed that "[African-Americans] are very strong." This response may be based on the fact that the Chinese youth watch a lot of NBA basketball games. Herein is a difference between Generation Y and the older generations in China: While the youths are more accepting of black people, many in the older generations are not. On the streets of the reputed tolerant, cosmopolitan Shanghai, the few African-Americans I saw were subject to conspicuous gawking by the local Chinese. China does not have much communication with these ethnic groups; the best interaction the Chinese have with African-Americans is through Western movies, which often portray blacks in a negative manner. It may be worth pointing out that Gen Y mostly envisions Americans as Caucasians, not African-Americans or Hispanics.

Gen Y is much more open-minded about other people than were their parents, and expect to see many more people from minority groups in the future.

Smoking

Smoking is a fad for not only China's youth, but also for the general population. Nearly 320 million people (a quarter of the population) smoke in the middle kingdom today.[17] Approximately 65 percent of the male population and seven percent of the female population smoke. The disparity between each

121

gender's smoking habits illustrates an important social norm, which holds that smoking is a man's sport. As my home-stay brother remarked one night, "Smoking is for men." The rules on smoking were formulated during the Cultural Revolution, when leaders branded female smoking a Western evil.

Now, however, female smoking has grown four percent in ten years, and the number of male and female smokers is expected to grow by at least three million annually, because the government's health committees do not place conspicuous warnings on cigarette packages and fail to heavily tax inexpensive cigarettes while incomes rise. The government owns the largest cigarette makers in the country and forces foreign importers to pay 65 percent tariffs on a brand like Marlboro. Smoking income is estimated to be one-tenth of total government revenue. But the healthcare system, which pays for most health costs of its citizens, is absorbing the annual three-quarter of a million fatalities. The government is attempting to decrease consumption by making it more difficult for firms to sell to juveniles.

Smoking is significant to Generation Y, as it is needed to socialize with others—already a difficult task. There are not many laws protecting Generation Y from smoking nor significant education programs about its harms; there are few incentives like excise taxes to deter smoking. Moreover, cigarette consumption is expected to increase as income rises and cigarette firms fight for a share of the market through advertising and price-cutting. By sponsoring important sporting events and educational institutions, these companies have already built solid brand names with which Gen Y is very familiar.

Life during Modernization

Stepping into a large building, I wondered, "Where am I?" The place certainly looked familiar. What were these recognizable products all the people were gazing at? Why did all these people wear smiles on their faces as they looked at these products? Ah ha! It was a Western-style supermarket.

For a brief moment my eyes deceived me and I thought I was in America. After all, such a thought is not too far off: the store sold high-tech refrigerators, vacuum cleaners, electronics, toys, and other products that a Western family would not do without.

Life in China's eastern metropolises resembles the rapid development in the 1950s in the United States. In cities such as Shanghai, more and more people are enjoying the benefits of a growing free market as more and more people obtain knowledge-based jobs from foreign corporations. As a result, a small but growing number of people are living the lifestyle of middle-class Westerners. This prosperity has been noticed not only by the countless tourists who rave about the skylines of Chinese cities, but also corporations that once were reluctant to sell in China. Designer clothing lines once refused to sell their products in China as a result of its notorious reputation of piracy and lack of a strong consumer base, as well as the economic obstacles of selling European goods in a country with a devalued currency. However, clothiers such as Louis Vuitton, Boss, Chanel, and Gucci have entered the China market by setting up shops in Shanghai, Beijing, and even smaller cities. The most plausible reason to enter the market is to create brand loyalty and satiate the demand for high quality clothing by wealthy executives.

Luxury and standard car manufacturers, also reluctant to sell vehicles in China due to governmental obstacles and previously low demand, are entering China's market in hopes of making it the largest car market in the world. Owners are happily driving their new vehicles on newly built freeways that are similar to America's freeways in the 1950s and 60s. On a macroeconomic level, a burgeoning bourgeoisie with cars allows individuals with newly earned wealth to take vacations. Families are now vacationing at beaches in Qingdao and Zhujiajian (Zhejiang province). To Americans or Europeans, vacations are second nature, often mandated by governmental policy. To the Chinese, however, the science of vacation is virtually as unknown and innovative as commercial space travel is to Americans. Some vacationers will come to the serene beaches but be unsure about how to spend their time; they will instinctively spend their vacation in their rooms, working. It is only in the next several decades that the Chinese will acculturate and accept vacationing.

Families now have to buy houses without the help of the government and pay mortgages and medical bills not covered by the government. In 2004, the Chinese government inserted a clause in the constitution that protects private property.[18] New types of insurance and financial services will make life much more complicated for Gen Y when it enters the workforce. Though not a new phenomenon, patients in China need to pay for healthcare services no matter what; approximately one-third of the population was denied treatment because of lack of funds in one year alone.[19]

In spite of these new worries, Gen Y in urban Shanghai is excited about the new changes.

What are your attitudes on the present modernization level of Shanghai?

Wang L.: I like it.

Gao: I do like it. Compared with other countries, however, Shanghai has a long way to go.

Wang J.: It has developed very quickly.

—older females

Caught up in globalization, the youth are trying to find a synthesis between modern and traditional culture. It will be interesting to see how modern China's culture will change through the choices Gen Y makes in the next 30 years, and how Gen Y's choices will affect its relationship with traditional Chinese culture.

Though the living environments of the West and China have not been comparable for centuries, Chinese living conditions are quickly catching up, mimicking those of the West.

Notes

[1]Jun Jing, 2000, p. 97.

[2]http://www.sfgate.com/cgi-bin/article.cgi?file=/c/a/2004/08/08/MNGV384L8P1.DTL.

[3]Jun Jing, 2000, p. 98.

[4]Jun Jing, 2000, p. 128.

[5]Jun Jing, 2000, p. 129.

[6]Jun Jing, 2000, p. 22; p. 105—all food types for holidays from Jun Jing and c-c-c.org.

[7]http://news.bbc.co.uk/1/shared/spl/hi/asia_pac/02/china_party_congress/china_ruling_party/key_people_events/html/great_leap_forward.stm.

[8]http://www.chinadaily.com.cn/english/doc/2004-11/09/content_389967.htm.

[9]"China finds Western ways bring new woes," *USA Today,* May 19, 2004.

[10] Jun Jing, 2000, p. 203.

[11]http://app1.chinadaily.com.cn/star/2000/1222/cn3-1.html.

[12]http://www.chinadaily.com.cn/english/doc/2004-10/13/content_381947.htm.

[13]http://www.chinahighlights.com/travelguide/bike.htm.

[14]http://www.chinanowmag.com/fastfact/fastfact.htm.
    —copyrighted.

[15]AMCHAT. August 2004, 13.

[16]http://www.disasterrelief.org/Disasters/971126worldbank/

[17]http://news.bbc.co.uk/1/hi/world/asia-pacific/770808.stm.

[18]http://news.bbc.co.uk/2/hi/asia-pacific/3509850.stm.

[19]http://www.asianresearch.org/articles/1747.html.

Chapter 6

Dreams and Development

C hina's Generation Y teenagers are focused on the future, having already devoted the first two decades of their lives in preparation. The youth are overwhelmingly pragmatic, and their dreams show how motivated they will be in their careers. They realize the only vehicle to success is through the modern, capitalist economy, which they mostly support. Moreover, Gen Y teenagers are now more cognizant of the similarities and differences between their parents' dreams for them and their own.

Though their dreams are sometimes either tenuous at best or too outlandish for reality, dreams provide an insight into the way China's youth have evolved from different generations. In reality, the youth have adapted their lives by accepting the modern marketplace as the way to fulfill their dreams, and are very pragmatic, especially in the long run, about their careers. For the first time in generations, many dreams are emerging in contexts almost completely different from the dreams of their parents. However, the perennial dream of trying to make a better life for their parents and themselves still remains ingrained in the minds of the youth. The youth's dreams should not only be looked on with interest, but also as a hint on the possible direction in which China and the world may be headed.

Career

The dreams that concern Gen Y the most are those relating to a career. Career success entails earning large sums of money and is predominantly envisioned as a white-collar occupation requiring a university degree. Dream jobs often conflict with more pragmatic occupations necessary for survival, and parents have at least some influence in the consideration of careers.

What do you want to do for your career?

Jiang, 17: My parents hope that I go to a university and be a governmental official in the future. I feel I'm quite confused.

Han, 17: I'm learning painting, so I want to be a cartoon designer.

Xu, 16: I haven't decided yet. Maybe a boss.

Qin, 16: To be a DJ.

Cheng, 17: My parents don't have many requirements for me. I wish to be the editor of game magazines.

Sun, 17: My parents don't have any expectations for me.

Yang, 16: My parents would like me to do whatever I want. I hope to be a journalist or someone who deals with writing; maybe a teacher.

Q&A with older males:

What are your dreams?

Xu W.: I want to be an engineer.

Xu J.: Superstar.

Wang X.: The same. In music.

Zhan W.: I want to be a network supervisor.

Q&A with Jiang Qin, M, 18 years old:

What do you dream about becoming? What about your future?

The future? I would like to start a company or something—a small company.

What type of business?

I haven't thought about it before. I mean to start a company with a partner.

What else?

A good father. A healthy person. A person who can get along really well with his friends.

Most of the careers specified by the youth have been created by China's move to a capitalist economy and foreign trends. How else would numerous teenagers learn about McDonald's franchising, entrepreneurship, cartoon designers, game designers, and music superstardom and seek to make them their careers? Three teenagers aspire to be doctors, basing their decision to study medicine on the will of their parents. Those who want to be engineers have no idea in which area of engineering they hope to specialize.

The great majority of males want to venture into business, a field especially enticing to the youth because it provides an easier way to earn money and wear the prestigious white collar. But when asked which area of business, the future merchants did not know which field they wished to enter. Although men were not sure where they would be in 10 years and what they would be doing, they knew that they would be better off than their parents.

What are the five most important parts of your life?

Friends, family, study, music, and money.

Why do you think money is very important?

Because it is the basis of everything. If you have money, you can do lots of things. For instance, when you go out with friends, you need money.

—Gu Y.

Nearly all the teens planned to marry in the future and all of the females planned to have a child, despite their tenuous plans for the future. Though marriage is of primary concern to individuals currently in their twenties, Gen Y will soon have to find spouses within a short period of courtship. It is important to note that marriage for university students in China used to be legal only after the couple graduated from university. In fact, the university could expel students for marrying, as teachers can punish children for dating during high school. Although marriage is still strongly discouraged by the schools' administrations, seventy universities have allowed students to marry since 2003.[1] The government also says that students do not need permission from employers to marry as couples did in the past.

When do you plan to marry?

Wang L.: 26.

Huang: Legal age.

Zhang Y.: I'm quite young now. I don't know what I will be doing in the future. I can't even imagine it. It is hard to tell if I will get married. I would only get married if I became successful in a career.

So will Gen Y's marriage patterns be different from those of their parents? Traditional ideas about marriage will still supersede Western ideas. Parents are consulted when a young couple plans to marry, although parents will not arrange marriages. However, in all probability the divorce rate will continue to climb as it tends to do in more developed nations.

The females have a grasp of certainty on their own future dreams. Females dream of driving their own European sports cars (no thoughts of soccer moms with minivans in their minds). Because females are generally more closely controlled by their parents, they mostly preferred traditional occupations that a mother and father would guide a child to follow.

Do you often communicate with your parents? What would they want you to do? Is there any difference between your thoughts and theirs?

Zhang: My parents want me to go to a university and afterwards find a good job.

What do your parents want you to do in the future?

Zhang: Be a doctor, but I don't want to be a doctor.

What do you want to be?

Zhang: A teacher.

Huang: Parents always want their children to find a good job, but I am not interested.

What kind of job is a good job?

Huang: One with a high salary.

Gao: I want to be a fashion designer, and my parents support me.

"I have no specific dreams. I just want to do what I want to do in my life."

The lack of motivation and indifference to the future of many of China's Gen Y are very perplexing problems to parents and elders who care very much about the future of their little emperors. The roots of these troubles lie in the environment surrounding the youth. School entrance exams that determine not only which university one will attend, but also if one will be able to attend university, and cutthroat competition because of high unemployment create a situation of uncertainty about the future. Accordingly, the youth choose occupations not based on ideology or personal satisfaction, but based on the possibility to gain the most economic flexibility for a more certain future. Parents firmly understand the reality of the situation and emphasize the acceptance of a particular job, even if the job does not ideologically suit the child. Because of filial piety, children obey in hopes of giving back generous gifts to those who nurtured them. The teens' streaks of creativity most likely originate from the Internet and television and essentially are freedom from the stifling system.

Travel and Living Abroad

Where will you live ten years from now, Shanghai or somewhere overseas?

Ye: Overseas.

Where?

Zhang: I want to live in Hong Kong.

Wang L.: England.

Huang: Korea.

Qiu: Germany.

Ye: I have no fixed destination. It's hard to decide what will happen after ten years.

Gao: Taiwan.

Wang J.: Australia.

Older males:

Will you live in Shanghai or overseas or another city in China?

Yang: Shanghai.

Xu W.: Abroad.

Wang J.: Both. I can stay in Shanghai as well as abroad. I think Shanghai is pretty good.

Wang X.: Japan.

In contrast to previous generations, Gen Y wants to travel around the world and live abroad, perhaps adding to the approximately 34 million Chinese who currently live abroad.[2] In 2004 alone, the number of trips taken abroad by Chinese nationals reached 29 million.[3] In many cases, the reasons for wishing to live in a country were simply predicated on the country's manufacturing of a product with which the teens were familiar. In addition, teens wished to move overseas to developed countries because of their modern facilities, their perceived better quality of life, and the skills that Gen Y teens can import back to China. Cheng (M, 17) is passionate about living in Japan: "My major is Japanese and I'd like to go to Japan after my three-year term is over because I feel games in Japan are quite developed. I'm almost a game master; I'd like to play every kind of game, and I have tried most of the games already."

There was one die-hard fan of America whose views did not particularly go over well in communist China.

Where do you want to live in the future?

America, overall. The construction of the city is better; the living environment is good, and this is the most important. I want to leave.

This anomalous teen not only wanted to change the education system like most of the respondents, but he also wanted to "change the nation—change federalism. I want the nation to be like America and learning would be the way to change it. Learning is better in foreign nations. Now the environment in China is bad because the corruption is bad." Another teen behind him jumped in and asserted that he would change the welfare system for the better as well.

Gen Y teens want to travel around the world to see the destinations that they studied in their stifling classrooms and Internet Web pages. Their penchant for travel signifies a new generation, one not limited by the borders of socialist-block countries, but by their interests tickled by textbooks, Internet, and stories of distant places. The youth often yearn to go places where people around them have been. For instance, one female mentioned she longed to travel to Tibet because her teacher had visited once and showed her class pictures of the trip. There exists a belief that people enter others' lives for a reason, and therefore youth have a tendency to follow the path others have taken. For instance, Mr. and Mrs. Zheng told their son to follow exactly what I did. To them, specifically the parents, I was his older brother and teacher. Teenagers also take interest outside of the realm of studying from media documentaries on CCTV and especially articles on exotic locations on a large Web portal's travel sections (sina.com.cn). What happened to the pervasive xenophobia we were all led to believe existed?

World Map Diagram of Desired Travel Destinations

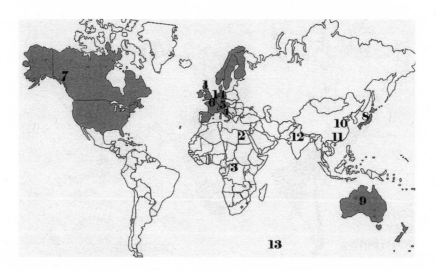

1. England
2. Egypt
3. The Congo
4. Italy
5. Austria
6. France

7. California

8. Japan

9. Australia

10. Suzhou

11. Hangzhou

12. India

13. South Pole

14. Germany

Wait, Why Not America?

It is difficult for many people to imagine wanting to go anyplace other than the United States of America. Its average annual salary makes it the second richest in the world next to Luxembourg. America has historically donated generous sums of money to poorer countries and the countries it nearly conquers. Consequently, the United States was the most beloved country in the world, viewed as the protector of freedom, democracy, and happiness. Today the situation seems quite different from travel abroad and from news programs. The Chinese, whom many Americans envision as destitute and toiling on rice patties, do not necessarily want to live in the Land of Opportunity.

The Chinese often see a distorted view of the United States through America's sometimes raunchy Hollywood movies portraying a society with poverty, racism, and a high crime rate. Though China is famed for its human rights violations, poverty, and numerous other problems, the Chinese would probably laugh at the hypocrisy and recall the Abu Graib scandal and Guantanamo Bay detention center's violation of human rights. Moreover, after September 11 and the country's strict immigration laws, few Chinese citizens have been able to afford to travel or receive visas to enter the U.S., in contrast to other developed nations. Exemplary Chinese students who can attend any university are choosing to study in Europe because of the lack of restrictions, and consequently those countries' economies benefit from the students' skills and advanced knowledge.

This is not to say the Chinese do not see any benefits from going to the U.S. or dislike the country itself. To them, American life is fast-paced and comfortable. Many mentioned that life in America was "freer" and "more comfortable." Gu Y., an anomalous teenager outspoken for his candid remarks on the future in China, declared:

...So that's why when I get married and have a kid, I will have him first go to elementary school and middle school in China, then make him go to college in the U.S. I will let him develop his individuality. This way he will have lots more room to develop.

—Gu Y.

A Peek into the Future

It is of little doubt that China as a whole will become modernized in the future. Not only will China boast some of the world's largest megacities, but it will also be able to boast better living conditions for its 800 million rural residents. Business executives around the world rant and rave about the construction in Shanghai and the city's competitive threat to Hong Kong and, to a growing extent, Tokyo.

The strength of the Chinese economy lies in its large population that will allow the country to support the older population and in its welfare system for the impoverished if worker productivity is increased. Chinese students are highly educated and can become more efficient and knowledgeable in working in the numerous foreign joint ventures. The Chinese economy can withstand the burden of social welfare for older generations in contrast with the Gen Ys of other developed nations.

In the next 500 years, China's development will be absolutely better than that in the U.S., because its potential for development is enormous. Why do foreign companies want to invest in China? It's because of China's potential. China has a population of 1.3 billion people. This population is a great resource; this potential has not yet been developed.

—Gu Y.

Charles Merkle of CBC Research in Shanghai argues that China will become a vast consumer economy in the future, one in which the ever-growing Chinese buying power will be large enough to consume its own and foreign goods. To do so, China must integrate its economy by ensuring that local economies have access to basic jobs (for instance, a McDonald's on every street corner and a Wal-Mart in every town), and must invest in sufficient infrastructure countrywide to attract investment to remote areas. To prop up individual incomes, the government must absorb all foreign investment and must not make any missteps along the way; today's economic growth is absolutely crucial to the country's future development.

When China succeeds in building a middle class of consumers, corporations will be able to continue to sell their products, and the living standards will increase for millions. If the government continues to relax its laws on businesses, more individuals will become entrepreneurs and become rich. Already the Chinese government is taking steps to cultivate a nascent bourgeoisie, estimated to be 40 percent of the population by 2020, by allowing individual investment in the Shanghai Stock Exchange and encouraging entrepreneurship. Members of this class could afford weekend vacations and purchase more appliances and clothing. With the multitude of people and China's obsession with education, Chinese families will devote more of their resources to educating their children, and the country will surpass many nations economically. But in order to accelerate such growth, the government will leave behind the rural peasants in exchange for larger shopping malls and towers. So far, the gap has widened even further, prompting sociologists to brand China as having one of the highest socioeconomic gaps in the world.[4]

China already is and will continue to be a huge player in the global market, with Shanghai at the helm in the foreseeable future. China's staggering number of cars ensures that China will be one of the greatest energy consumers in the world, rivaling the United States and driving up prices around the world. Diplomatically, the world is China's world. China remains a major force in the United Nations by holding a permanent seat on the Security Council. China is also the puppet master of maintaining peace in East Asia because it has control over the outbreak of war with Taiwan. It also has leverage with the U.S. because China helps in negotiations with the North Korean government; its corporations lobby on behalf of the Chinese government with other governments around the world.

The aforementioned factors may seem oversimplified when juxtaposed with the nation's problems. China's legal system is underdeveloped, opaque, and full of holes, making it more difficult to construct a free market economy in China. China must maintain efficiency in spite of traditional *guanxi* relations and reduce unemployment in the face of massive layoffs in state-run corporations to make them more competitive. The government also faces the huge task of diminishing one of the world's largest socioeconomic gaps between the rich and the poor. In spite of these obstacles, Chinese youth optimistically anticipate improvements in China, and predict that China will be economically better off than the U.S. in the next twenty years as it becomes a developed country.

With the advent of capitalism and equality in the workforce, women can attain the same status and wealth as men, leading some to believe that their social roles will change. Gen Y females generally admired the fact that China was traditional and maybe their roles would be more equal, whereas males believed that the more ambitious females would eventually earn more money than they. One female said, "I think men should do the housework and take care of the children." A few of the older males mentioned that they would accept that their wives earned more than they did. The majority, however, hoped and felt confident that the current gender roles would not change significantly. Female Gen Yers still remain traditional in their views on family and gender roles:

Do you think twenty years from now that men and women will play different roles in their daily life and work?

Huang: I think men should do the housework in the family. In addition, they should take care of the children.

Zhang: I don't think it will change a lot. No big change.

For instance, in what aspect will women be a leader, or in what aspect will men be a leader in the family? Then what about in work?

Wang L.: It'll be similar to the situation today; namely, that women focus more on family while men focus less.

Gao: I think women should focus more on family while men should focus more on career. If I as a woman earn more than a man, I won't choose him. In the family, women should pay more attention to finance. As far as a career, I think men should be more successful than women.

Do you wish him to do a better job in his career?

Gao: Yes. The reason is that if you want to create a family, the man's income must be higher than the woman's. Then a family can be created. Men can't rely on women.

Their reluctance to change family interpersonal relations indicates how important Chinese culture and tradition are to the youth in spite of all the changes occurring around them.

Older males, most of whom do not plan on ever leaving Shanghai, also feel China's future will get better. They all noted some trends for the betterment of China, especially the prospect of fewer people. Other trends that they expected were improved infrastructure and transportation, better telecommunications, and a more powerful economic outlook. They noted the importance or inevitability of a healed relationship with Taiwan, the elimination of superfluous jobs in state-owned companies to compete with Western companies, and the implementation of social and economic reforms that place men and women on an equal footing. The group expressed varying opinions when it came to men and women in the workforce. For example, one male said that he would be comfortable if his wife earned more than he did. Another person disagreed, saying: "It shouldn't be like that. You see, if a woman has skills and you marry her, you have larger skills." This older male group was probably the most vocal of the four groups when it came to the future of their country.

The youth are familiar with "Western-style" villas in Shanghai and hope to purchase them if they can afford it. The teenagers overwhelmingly seek to reform the ostensibly negative aspects of Chinese culture, such as spitting, pushing, and littering, and also wish to see a better organized modernization of China. Fully cognizant of the implications of modernization, the youth realize that modernization benefits yet also harms their country.

Entrepreneurship

With relaxed market regulations and China's membership in the WTO, entrepreneurship is flourishing. The best route to accomplish their dreams of getting rich quick is entrepreneurship, and there is no doubt that China's Generation Y will produce millions of entrepreneurs.

Yu Q., who will matriculate at a university, plans to open a bar by herself; she learned how to be an entrepreneur through her mother's establishment of an interior design store. Several male teens wanted to open their own McDonald's franchises. They probably have heard about one foreign-born Chinese entrepreneur, Meng Sun, who started her own restaurant in Tianjin. Her story is quite appealing to would-be entrepreneurs, for she ironically once worked as an hourly McDonald's employee in Calgary, Canada, while attending the University of Calgary, and has since become a successful franchisee. It should be noted that Meng Sun had to have had significant resources prior to the venture, as she had to come up with $300,000 for the initial purchase of the franchise.[5] McDonald's is looking to rapidly expand in the Chinese market and has received 500 applications from prospective entrepreneurs to run new restaurants. KFC expanded its franchises with the work of 55 lucky entrepreneurs who paid the large sum of approximately $970,000 to gain franchising rights. Since 1987, the brand has opened its 1,000[th] KFC in China, which is located in Beijing.[6] But for many of Gen Y, franchising is out of the question because only individuals who have enough capital can establish their own franchises.

Young adults find that their success lies in the Internet. Wang Shan of Hangzhou, a young fashion designer, has capitalized on pop Japanese trends by creating a website that sells COSPLAY gear and costumes. She has started a shop that sells costumes for youth engaged in contests and enjoyment. She has been contacted by a firm to export her costumes to Japan, the origin of the fad.[7]

One couple decided to capitalize on the increasingly popular fad of Western weddings. Chen Tao, a student in Shanghai, got the idea to bring the fad to his original hometown in Sichuan province from a Western wedding he attended in Shanghai. When he saw the enthusiasm of the town for the wedding, he decided to establish his own wedding agency with his wife. Now he handles the preparations for Western weddings for 600 couples and his company has grown to 30 employees.[8] The Western fad is opening a vast market for other entrepreneurs to enter.

Most of the successful entrepreneurs are young individuals who use Western fads and fuse them with Chinese tradition. This further underscores the fact that China will not become purely Westernized like America and Europe. On the contrary, it will become more like Japan, a country that has embraced modernization but retained its own characteristics.

Dreams are one of the greatest indicators of Gen Y's future; they exemplify the optimistic spirit of the generation and the youth's potential driven by their ambition. Dreams may fluctuate and change like the markets, but the generation's ambition to ameliorate their lives and those of their family will remain implanted in them forever. Prior to the influx of Westernization, individual dreams were not tolerated and went unfulfilled; but as Gen Y embraces Western prosperity, Western values, and relaxed laws, the individual will fulfill more of his/her own goals, not solely those of others.

Other Influences on the Development of China

The Chinese youth are well aware of the implications of modernization their country faces. Advancing the Chinese society and economy comes at a cost to their countrymen's quality of life and to their own. To them, the influences that will affect the development of China and thus their aforementioned dreams are:

♦ Education—literacy
♦ Deforestation
♦ Overpopulation
♦ Natural disasters—earthquakes, floods

- War with Taiwan
- Increase in pollution
- High-tech industries (IT technology)
- Judicial corruption
- Strength of the military
- Changing family roles
- Foreign firms vs. state-owned companies
- Better transportation
- Unemployment

Gen Y believes that China's education system will be the key to its development. Nearly all teens mentioned that high-tech jobs would increase in the future and bring prosperity to China. Cutthroat competition and few positions at universities drive companies to China for cheap, yet intelligent workers. Though they realize that their education system has problems, they believe that they have learned more through their education system than American youth. Gen Y encourages curriculum reforms that will encourage creativity and accelerate national development.

Deforestation will soon create ecological problems in China as people fell trees. Deforestation allowed the Yangtze River to expand and flood outlying areas, killing 2,500 people. This devastation acted as a wake-up call by forcing the government to enact green ordinances; deforestation is by no means a solution to China's growing need for timber. One environmental agency believes that China is currently consuming illegally harvested timber through a smuggling ring that carries about 300,000 cubic meters of wood from Indonesia to Zhangjiagang.[9] It claims China's supply of timber can only supply half of the nation's growing demand. [15]

The economic explosion occurring in China is causing vast impending socioeconomic gaps in Chinese society that are affecting China's youth. Adults working in the eastern, coastal cit-

143

ies are earning significantly more than their compatriots in remote China. Nearly 100 million Chinese, largely based in the poor, western areas of the nation, earn under $1.00 a day. Consequently, throngs of immigrants from inner China are attempting to find lucrative employment in the cities, but are too poor to relocate. Because the educational system in China is exceptionally demanding, the majority of rural citizens are unable to afford or work toward a full education and thereby ascend the social ladder. Some rural workers, also known as *mingong*, are able to find migrant worker jobs, but they are unable to share the same welfare benefits as city dwellers. Moreover, the gap carries on into healthcare, where the government pays thirteen times the amount for urban residents than for rural residents, who compose 80 percent of the Chinese population ($10.37 for rural, $130 for urban).[10]

Analysts have speculated that the central government has devoted its attention to the economic prosperity of its eastern cities to prevent a rebellion, which would be devastating for the government. Though the implications for the disparity are unknown, the situation of the haves and have-nots will either remain stable or worsen, as welfare funds are spent to subsidize the colossal growth in cities. The looming situation will probably not escalate into a rebellion because the government would be able to quickly suppress the uprising or implement economic reforms.

On the other hand, those living in the eastern areas of the country are enjoying unprecedented economic prosperity and an atmosphere of hope, once thought by intellectuals to be forever lost. Chinese cities in the East are experiencing the economic prosperity that America exhibited in the 1950s. Children and adults have expressed their elation over new stores like Wal-Mart, Carrefour, and numerous Western-style department stores. It is at these stores that mothers buy household appliances and children buy high-tech materials. This picture is remarkably similar to the 1950s in America; it could dramatically change if the government makes a mistake.

China's youth accept and understand that their country is unique in the government's regulation of the number of births allowed. Overpopulation in their eyes not only causes problems that work against their country's prosperity, but increases competition, ensuring that they must work even more diligently to be secure economically.

Gen Y's Feuds and Political Beliefs

The youth harbor some political beliefs molded by their parents, government, the news they read on the Internet, and other influences. The conflicts and grudges have the potential to considerably threaten China's development and will ultimately play a larger role in politics as China becomes more economically powerful. It is thus imperative for us to understand the youth's perspective on regional conflicts.

China's youth are patently against other nations going to war. However, it is difficult to know whether they are against nations other than the U.S. to be engaged in war. They yearn for peace unless Chinese interests are threatened, as in the highly tumultuous crisis with Taiwan.

During the late 1940s, two million Chinese fled the nation to the island of Taiwan as China's communist party battled the Chinese nationalist army. Over the years Taiwan's economy has become one of the most successful in Asia. China is restating its claim over the island in a "One China" policy. Propaganda is often spread on both sides as both militaries purportedly "prepare for war." Though Generation Y is sure that it is only a matter of time, it appears that Gen Y will not be impetuous, for it understands the large-scale implications of such a war. Like many international observers, the teenagers believe that a war could spark huge problems for the United States and Japan, among others. The United States would be torn between the two be-

145

cause it has historically maintained good ties with democratic Taiwan along with new investment ties with communist China. Japan would also be caught in the turmoil because of its historic and cultural affinity to Taiwan after having dominated the island from 1895 to 1945 and assimilated its people to the Japanese way of life.[11] Japan subtly hints that it would support Taiwan militarily in a potential war and has recently deemed China as a "concern." Beijing officials believe that Japan is disobeying constitutional restrictions that prevent Japan's involvement in military conflicts. From an economic standpoint, the lack of American, European, Japanese, and even Taiwanese investment funds in China in the event of a war could spell economic disaster during this crucial period of China's industrialization, not to mention the military implications. The incessant propaganda on both sides will undoubtedly formulate the ideas of China's youth on the issue and, perhaps, the outcome of the conflict in the years to come.

The situation seemed to worsen in March 2005 when China ratified the Anti-Secession law, giving it the right to use force to prevent any region from becoming independent, though a head Chinese official states that force would be a "last resort."[12] The law is likely to slow Taiwanese investment in China, now estimated at $100 billion.[13] Moreover, it may prevent the Europeans from disobeying arms sanctions imposed after the 1989 Tiananmen Square demonstrations.[14] China is most likely using the law and its bombastic gestures to prevent secession at all costs rather than as an excuse for war.

Many teens were quite opinionated when it came to Taiwan and its long-standing feud with China. Daily propaganda points to a "One China Policy" that advocates the inclusion of democratic, capitalist Taiwan with communist China. Likewise, one teen proclaimed, "Generally speaking, I think the Mainland bears responsibility for the government of Taiwan." Another added, "I think the attitude of the Chinese government is not tough enough." They are certain that Taiwan will become one with China eventually upon stronger force from the Chinese government.

Nearly all of the teens abhor the nation of Japan. Their parents and government inculcated in them the "unforgivable act" that Japan committed in World War II against China known as the "Rape of Nanjing." The Japanese imperial army invaded China in 1937; after wresting control of Shanghai it marched to Nanjing. When the locals did not leave as asked, the imperial army massacred some 300,000 people, raped 20,000 to 80,000 women, and committed other atrocities.[15] Likewise, the teenagers exclaimed that the Japanese military invaded China, massacred their countrymen in Nanjing, and raped their grandmothers. Not only that, they exclaimed, but the Japanese never really or sincerely apologized for their actions, unlike Germany. The feud is fueled by a controversy over the way in which the events in Nanjing are portrayed in Japanese school textbooks, which call the attack on unarmed civilians an "advance." Also fueling tensions is Japanese Prime Minister Junichiro Koizumi's yearly trips to the Yasukuni Shrine to pay homage to all of Japan's war casualties, including the convicted World War II criminals, a Japanese cabinet official's statement that belittled the war crimes as being bogus, and China's desire for more than a verbal apology despite seventeen verbal apologies by Japanese statesmen, including the emperor himself.

These wounds run deep for the youth who certainly showed their political opinions at the August 2004 Asian Soccer Cup held in four Chinese cities. Many fans, including Chinese youth, participated in Japanese flag-burning, throwing bottles, booing during the singing of the Japanese national anthem, and rushing the Japanese team's bus. In fact, the situation was so bad in one city that 2,000 Japanese spectators had to wait two hours for the police to push back the mob.[16]

The anger in the youth is further fueled by the Chinese government, schools, and parents. One Gen Yer explained that his teachers had stressed to him for years that Japan committed "an unforgivable act" against China and that he should thus hate Japan. Gu Y. had an opportunity to intern at a Japanese firm. He replied that he hated Japanese people until he worked with them in an office environment, whereupon he realized that it is the Japanese government, and not the people of Japan, that is culpable for the Nanjing Massacre. Similar to the Chinese government, the Chinese youth adamantly seek an apology from Japan and are quick to mention the textbook controversy.[17]

Ironically, however, the history of Nanjing does not deter the Chinese youth from purchasing and preferring Japanese products. As mentioned before, China's Gen Y is unable to link its hatred for Japan with Japanese products. On the contrary, the Chinese adore and prefer Japanese products.

The government fuels the hatred but silences it when Japanese officials visit Beijing. It has allegedly encouraged a large-scale petition headed by a Chinese website that has received 22 million signatures protesting Japan's potential inclusion into the U.N. Security Council. The U.S. supports Japan's inclusion, thereby hurting relations between it and China.[18] However, the major points of contention between Japan and China will be concentrated on the seas, where China is testing its submarines, searching for oil in the Pacific Ocean, and contesting territory claims.

Some years ago university students who were several years older than Gen Y were furious at American foreign policy. This is to be expected from youth heavily influenced by propaganda that attempts at every blunder to point out America's pugnacious foreign policy. Many young teenagers have not forgotten America's 1999 bombing of the Chinese embassy in Yugoslavia, believing that the bombing was not an error. After the bombing, youth took to the streets, angrily protesting and demanding an apology. Protesters angrily scoffed at any Westerners who happened to be present near the demonstration sites. University students also witnessed the backlash that ensued with the capturing of the American spy plane on China's Hainan Island in April 2001, and followed closely America's decision to arm Taiwan with advanced weapons. China's youth are keenly aware of the political measures taken by President Bush for the war in Iraq.

The younger girls and younger males, in particular, were the most knowledgeable in regard to politics because their school's curriculum is more flexible and allows them to learn about politics. The younger girls were quite verbal about their opposition to the war in Iraq and specifically mentioned that the Bush administration is a catastrophe for America.

Thus a pattern emerges with Chinese youth. They do not have the ability to separate their perceived notions of a country from their product preferences. Generation Y will not pour French wine down city sewers if their government gets into a scuffle with France. The youth still prefer products from the U.S. and Japan in spite of their intense hatred for the past errors and foreign policy of those countries.

Gen Yers did not mention the conflict in the north with the Korean peninsula, but it has great importance in the development of China and the quality of life of the youth. China has leverage in making North Korea obey America's demands but it has little incentive to do so. China does not want the regime to fall because it would weaken communism, cause a diaspora of North Koreans into China, and hint to other critics of the Chinese government that they can succeed in altering China's foreign policy.[19] On a grander scale, a major conflict between North Korea and Western countries would not bode well for Gen Y, who would be inherently close to the conflict; but in the aftermath of a fallen North Korea, the region could see the emergence of a healthier East Asia, one that could even see investment into the northern peninsula.

It is tempting to see the Association of Southeast Asian Nations (ASEAN), the major conglomeration of Asian countries, becoming a major force in China's Generation Y's lifetime. As a group, ASEAN boasts 500 million people and three-fourths of a trillion dollars in combined GDP, sounding like an amazing economic powerhouse as a whole; however, the ideological differences and conflicts between nations are now too strong to unite members in one dynamic body like the EU. Not only do ASEAN members' political affiliations range from one side of the spectrum to the other, but the group also has ideological and economic differences that easily fragment members, unlike in the EU. America does not ardently support ASEAN because the bloc undermines its power in Asian politics; and as China becomes more powerful, its conflicts with its neighbors could severely weaken ASEAN.

China's military forces are rapidly growing. Military spending, at $30 billion in 2005, has increased officially by 12.6 percent this year, though other countries estimate the real military budget to be 30 to 50 percent more. China is working on mobile missile launchers that mount missiles with nuclear warheads (Dongfeng-31) on trucks that could potentially reach America's northwest, and is investing in feats such as in-air fueling. *The New York Times* states that the military is constructing twenty-three new marine ships and thirteen submarines.[20] The American government is quite cautious, as Peter Goss, Director of the CIA, mentioned that the Chinese military is prepared to invade Taiwan.

Should America be afraid? Though Peter Goss's words can be viewed as propaganda, the Chinese military buildup has the ability to affect America's defense of Taiwan. America should be alarmed at the rate China is amassing its forces because it is shifting the current balance of power in the region. Strategically, it should also be concerned about Europe's disregard for the sanctions, because Europe is overlooking the future implications of selling weapons and technology to a country that will fight a war for its unity and ideology. This technology could possibly give the Chinese military insight into the inner workings of the American military.[21] But again, this sizing up of the Chinese army is overblown, because the Chinese army is ill managed and still has significant catching up to do to become a major military power in the world. Americans will come to fear China if and when the conflict between Taiwan and China actually makes national news, and when Americans abruptly learn about the amount of power, both politically and economically, China has.

For me, politics was an unknown and exhilarating territory to delve into. Where were the "Death to the West" chants and communist proverbs that I had so foolishly been led to expect by my culture? The line of questioning was along the lines of legality, but I had to frequently verify that the questions asked to Gen Y were harmless. Younger teens were worried about talking politics:

What do you think about the Taiwan problem?

Can I say whatever I want to?... Generally speaking, I think the mainland bears responsibility for the government of Taiwan. It can't be interfering all the time, although some people on the island are against independence.

If we declare a war on Taiwan because of the Taiwan problem, I don't think it would be seen to be good by the world, since war will bring a very heavy impact to our country.

—Sun, 17

Some of the younger respondents still cast doubts about Japan.

"We still need to watch out for this country."
"It seems not so friendly to us, and it's threatening our economic situation."

Although the Chinese youth are conscious of the influences that will interfere with the development of China, they must learn through years of experience how to deal with and overcome these problems. They are well educated and observant young people who strive for a modern life and all the luxuries enjoyed by the Western world. In the immediate time horizon, both the Chinese government and Gen Y are intelligent enough not to let any interferences keep their country and economy from advancing.

China's Gen Y generally has either a neutral or auspicious opinion of the American people. On a personal note, I did not receive any angry remarks or insults from Chinese people—the same cannot be said for my travels in Europe—though I will say that I often heard *waiguoren* (foreigner) here and there. Inasmuch as the Chinese historically never forget anything and after the wake of the United States' bombing of an embassy, the relations are relatively peaceable.

Gen Y is the heir to China's optimistic future and political situation. As China amasses wealth and military might, it will become a giant in Asian politics. It already has a pivotal role in the Korean peninsula and enough conflicts with its neighbors to catalyze war and destabilize the region. But it is important to realize that many of the teenagers understand the broader implications of such wars, even though they may be for the conflicts.

Notes

[1] http://www.chinadaily.com.cn/english/doc/2005-03/30/content_429412.htm.

[2] http://www.berkeley.edu/news/berkeleyan/2002/11/20_chin.html.

[3] http://www.time.com/time/asia/covers/501050516/china_consumers2.html.

[4] *International Herald Tribune*, August. 2, 2004. Front page.

[5] "Chinese Entrepreneurs Eye Fast-Food Franchises," February 17, 2005, by Steven Gray and Geoffrey A. Fowler. http://www.entrepreneur.com/article/0,4621,320132,00.html.

[6] http://www.chinatoday.com.cn/English/e2004/e200406/p26.htm.

[7]http://www.china.org.cn/english/NM-e/68924.htm.

[8]http://www.chinadaily.com.cn/english/doc/2004-10/13/content_381947.htm.

[9]"Green Guise," *The Economist,* March 26, 2005, 42.

[10]http://www.asianresearch.org/articles/1747.html.

[11]http://en.wikipedia.org/wiki/Taiwan.

[12]http://www.washingtonpost.com/wp-dyn/articles/A15294-2005Mar7.html.

[13]http://www.bloomberg.com/apps/news?pid=10000080&sid=a7QiOVSmlLF4&refer=asia, other sources say differently.

[14]http://www.atimes.com/atimes/China/GC29Ad07.html.

[15]http://www.cnn.com/WORLD/9712/13/remembering.nanjing/

[16]http://www.cnn.com/2004/SPORT/football/08/07/football.china/

[17]http://www.economist.com/displaystory.cfm?story_id=3786409.

[18]http://www.nytimes.com/2005/03/31/international/asia/31cnd-china.html.

[19]*The Economist,* March 26, 2005, 11-12. Some, but not all, reasons for not going to war are taken from here.

[20]http://www.voanews.com/english/2005-03-23-voa76.cfm.

[21]http://news.bbc.co.uk/2/hi/americas/4342527.stm.

Chapter 7

Gen Y's Inherited Economy

China's youth will not only inherit large sums of money from their grandparents and parents, but also a rapidly changing, burgeoning marketplace. Indeed, many manufacturers are finding that they can make the same or higher profits in China than in the U.S, not because of individual large purchasing power, but because of the sheer volume of customers. The increasing purchasing power of today's teenagers and their familiarization with consumerism will continue to make them a dream to sellers in the global market. So profound is the opportunity in China that a record $61 billion of investment entered the country in 2004.[1] There are upward of half a million foreign invested ventures in China. An ASEAN trading state and a member of the World Trade Organization (WTO), China has become ASEAN's sixth largest trading partner.[2] Trade volume between China and other ASEAN states is increasing at 10 percent per year. The current developments in the marketplace are laying the foundation for China's position in the future and will have a huge effect on the prosperity of Gen Y and the growth of the Chinese middle class.

Each year, upward of 28 million babies are born in China, roughly half the population of France.[3] China's population will continue to grow by 10 million people annually until its peak of 1.46 billion in 2035.[4] The United Nations estimates that in just half a century the number of people older than fifty will be twice the number of people younger than twenty.[5] While the overall population is maturing, there still exists a ripe market of adolescents whose ranks will reach around 185 million in 2025.[6]

Of the 1.3 billion inhabitants of China, the total split be-tween males and females is essentially even, with 51 percent male and 49 percent female.[7] China's youth, age 10 to 14, boasts the most populated age segment in China, followed by the 35 to 39 age segment. In contrast, the most populated age segment in the U.S. is between the ages of 40 and 49. The following table sum-marizes China's population picture in 2000:[8]

China's Population by Age Segment

Age Group	Total	Male	Female	%
0 to 4	94,475,500	50,347,791	44,127,709	7.4
5 to 9	103,368,052	54,449,328	48,918,724	8.1
10 to 14	125,227,009	65,228,382	59,998,627	9.9
15 to 19	102,943,613	53,193,649	49,749,964	8.1
Total youth population	426,014,174	223,219,150	202,795,024	33.5
Total population	1,242,612,226	640,275,969	602,336,257	100

Source: U.S. Census Bureau, International Data Base.

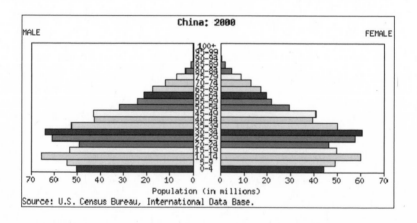

Although China's large population is a hindrance to indi-vidual high net worths, it is working to its advantage during the country's economic development. A larger youth population is important for China because it encourages foreign investment and pays for the welfare services of their parents. Because fewer jobs will be available as a result of downsizing of national corporations, the youth must become more productive and enhance the economy. When China's population peaks, the country will face problems of paying the high healthcare costs for the enormous older populations.

Indeed, these economic statistics and the favorable demographics of the fast growing youth population are eye-popping trends to Western providers of products and services. Marketers should realize that brand loyalty and reputation are crucial in Chinese teens' decision to purchase expensive goods, and building brand loyalty begins at early ages. A surprising number of corporations have either directly or largely targeted the exploding youth market in their marketing strategies, many establishing multimillion-dollar marketing plans. The corporations that understand this generation—their thoughts and preferences—are finding success with them. Consider the following examples:

♦ The NBA and Nokia have collaborated to offer the viewing of basketball games and sporting video games accessible on mobile phones.[9] Nokia sees the best way to gain market share in China, a rat race for its competitors, is to build its brand among the large youth population through support of one of the most popular sports among the youth. As part of its marketing strategy, Nokia is lending its support to *Basketball Without Borders,* which helps members of Gen Y to live healthy lives. Phillips Electronics also markets to the youth through its sponsorship of a university football league.

♦ Mary Kay launched an upscale "Timewise" cosmetics line aimed at young females and young white-collar females. Mary Kay, which entered the Chinese market in 1998 and had to do away with its direct-selling model because of governmental regulations, is doing phenomenally well, with annual sales that were reportedly close to one billion RMB in 2002. [10]

♦ Starbucks is rapidly expanding in China, operating more than 51 stores.[11] The president of Starbucks Asia-Pacific Group mentions that the company's marketing campaign is particularly aimed toward individuals between the ages of 18 and 30.[12]

♦ McDonald's is hoping to capitalize on the youth market with its opening of McKids stores in China, selling toys, modern apparel, and entertainment products.[13] Its advertisements, including the likes of Yao Ming and other celebrities, and "I'm lovin' it" campaign cater to the youth by showing contemporary young people enjoying the company's food. McDonald's has an aggressive expansion plan, opening at least 100 new stores a year in China over the next several years and exposing "Happy Meals" and Disney-theme promotions to millions of children.[14] The chain also attempts to curry favor with the entrepreneurial youth by allowing selected individuals to open their own franchised restaurants.

♦ KFC developed in 1995 an appealing figure called "Chicky" (*Qiqi*), a young Colonel Sanders, to woo the youth after the bland reception given to the traditional figure of Colonel Sanders.[15] KFC offers birthday party services and has become part of being a modern Gen Y teen in China. Because children and teenagers want to eat at KFC, parents will often succumb to their children's wants.

♦ Pizza Hut markets to young people in China by television advertising. In one commercial, a Chinese student jumped on his desk at school because of his pizza-pie craze, definitely delinquent behavior in Chinese culture. Ultimately, Pizza Hut's ad, similar to those of many other Western corporations, was deemed inappropriate by the government and was pulled from circulation.[16]

♦ One brand of Instant Noodles sought to entice the youth to purchase its product by including stickers that could be collected for a T-shirt.[17] Some children forced their parents to buy the noodles just to obtain the T-shirts.

China Misnomers

With the government decentralizing its power in hopes of becoming more efficient, along with China's entrance into the WTO, foreign firms can now take some respite in their problems with the central government. Foreign-held corporations and subsidiaries that in the past had to have an office in Beijing to communicate with the government can now communicate with less daunting provincial governments. Decentralization provides a multitude of better qualities for doing business, allowing for better enforcement of laws, competitive incentives for investment, fewer restrictions, less contact with inefficient bureaucratic workers, and thus less corruption.[18]

The Chinese government did not cause capitalism to flourish; it was the people entrenched in communism. A result of food shortages and survival skills, people living in collectives broke the government's stringent quotas and sold more of their production in free markets.[19] The prosperity swayed the government to ease its quotas and restrictions during the early part of the 1980s, allowing people to ameliorate their own situations.[20] With the help of individual participation in free enterprise, these reforms allowed China's intrinsic capitalist spirit to prosper.

A misconception about the shopping habits of Chinese citizens is that the tastes of all Chinese citizens are homogenous. There are distinct tastes in each of the provinces, and localization strategies to appeal to China's youth are business imperatives. For example, GM vehicles appeal to Shanghai car owners unlike the people in Hong Kong, who prefer Honda. As my home-stay brother contends, the Adidas brand is more popular in Shanghai because the Shanghainese are more sports-loving than people in other provinces. Much of KFC's success since its beginning in the China market in 1987 can be attributed to its restaurants' quick adaptation to each local market, virtually becoming a nonforeign part of the community and helping to lure parents. For example, KFC recently introduced several China-only chicken products that were customized to the regional food palates of Sichuan, Guangdong, and Beijing. The chain also lures teens and children by its foreign and modern atmosphere that dignifies them as a unique generation.

There was a long-standing belief that prime shopping in Asia was limited to Hong Kong or Japan, but that simply is not the case today. In just a few years Chinese cities like Shanghai and Beijing have become shopping "meccas" for consumers. In fact, Shanghai women, known for their business and fashion senses, are reputed to be trendy shoppers enamored with foreign and expensive clothing.

Employment

As more multinational companies enter the Chinese market, the demand for employees with localized knowledge will increase. Employment levels throughout China continue to expand and totaled 744.32 million people at the end of 2002, compared to 737.4 million at the end of 2001.[21] WTO membership suggests that overseas investments in China will continue to grow at exponential levels. However, China's transition from a planned economy to a significantly more capitalistic economy is causing some troubles for its people, including increased competition. Cumbersome state-owned firms cannot compete with more productive foreign companies that employ significantly fewer workers; consequently, they either merge with foreign companies or lay off hundreds of employees at inefficient, superfluous jobs. While approximately 12 million people in China lose their jobs annually, mostly due to more efficient production methods, only six million people are reemployed.[22] Officials mention that the government is working to curtail unemployment. Interestingly, the government used to recognize unemployment as a capitalistic problem, yet officials now use the term in policy.

Economists expect unemployment to increase in the future as the trend of rural workers relocating to cities becomes more pronounced and efficiency in production improves. Moreover, the large population of middle-aged people will greatly add to China's unemployment. As a result of the Cultural Revolution, many of the parents of Generation Y were forced to work with peasants in the countryside. Thus they do not have the necessary skills to work in China's competitive job market vis-à-vis younger and lower-paid workers.

Employment figures do not tell the real story facing people. Lauren Buckalew explains the plight of an unemployed worker: "The man was laid off because costs were too high, and the factory scaled down operations. For the record, labor is cheaper in China than equipment at present, so another human would have been his replacement, if that were the case, instead of scaling down. His case is particularly unfortunate because he married late in life, and was laid off around age 53 when his daughter was only a baby. He applied to the local neighborhood committee for help, a communist-style neighborhood watch group that deals with matters such as the 'one-child policy,' birth control information, activities for the elderly, etc.; unfortunately, the committee itself had no positions open and knew of none elsewhere."

It is unlikely that this unemployed man will find another job because his skills cannot compete with those of younger workers. The social safety net will not help him much because it is not strong enough to absorb the vast numbers of unemployed. The frustration that adults feel will undoubtedly affect their children and the future of the government.

What will our nation be like in 10 or 20 years?

Cheng: It should be better than the current situation. I think the rich are getting richer while the poor are getting poorer. Polarization. The main reason is because people who are around 40 to 50 years old now haven't been to college before. They don't have the academic credentials, so they have to be laid off. Twenty years later, these people are going to be very old, so there won't be so many (people) laid off among our generation. I don't think that there will be many (socioeconomic) differences between people in the future.

Gen Y is surprisingly optimistic about its future in the competitive job market, viewing office towers and more individual prosperity as the major indicators of a better job market. Though they may embark on more modern careers, the problem will still be largely present during their young adulthood.

Employers of business and high-tech companies face human resource issues such as keeping quality employees. An expatriate entrepreneur in China indicated that when another company or head-hunting firm approaches a valuable employee, that employee will almost always accept the more lucrative offer.

Income

A middle-class family has a monthly income of at least 6,200 RMB ($750), and a low-income family would be one that earns less than 3,000 RMB ($360). According to FriedlNet, the living standards in both urban and rural areas of China are improving. The annual per capita disposable and inflation-adjusted income for urban households stood at 7,703 RMB ($963) in 2002, an increase of 13.4 percent from 2001. Even the per capita income of rural households increased 4.8 percent the same year, to 2,476 RMB ($300). Also, the ranks of Chinese inhabitants in rural areas that were considered to be living in poverty have declined. This figure stood at 28.2 million in 2002, a decrease of 1.07 million from 2001 levels.

The following table in RMB summarizes the income improvements in urban and rural areas of China, along with the corresponding declines in Engel Coefficients (the proportion of food expenditures to total household expenditures). The percentage declines are clear barometers of the fact that households in both locales are realizing higher disposable incomes.[23] Ultimately, the numbers indicate that living conditions have improved in China.[24]

	2002	2001	2000	1999	1998
Disposable Incomes*	7703.00	6860.00	6280.00	5854.00	5425.00
Per Capita Incomes**	2476.00	2366.00	2253.00	2210.00	2162.00
Engel Coefficient*	37.7%	37.9%	39.2%	41.9%	44.5%
Engel Coefficient**	46.2%	47.7%	49.1%	52.6%	53.4%

* urban areas

** rural areas

A key component of China's income structure is the considerable increase in the amount of money that teenagers now carry and spend. One study reported that the average monthly allowance for middle school students in 15 major cities was about $10, and that children often represent 50 percent of the family expenditure in major cities. Another indicates that youth in four large Chinese cities received an average monthly allowance of 121 RMB ($15).[25] These amounts increase with age and have increased in recent years.

Cities and Provinces

China has the third largest land area in the world and boasts the largest population. Provinces not only vary in culture, but also in development. There are twenty-two provinces (excluding Taiwan), five autonomous regions, four municipalities directly under the control of the Central Government, plus the special administrative regions of Hong Kong and Macao. It is evident that most of the country's economic growth is powered by Shanghai, Beijing, Hong Kong, and other eastern coastal cities, especially those that over the years have benefited from their status as Special Economic Zones (SEZ). Clearly, Gen Yers in these eastern, prosperous cities are much more apt to purchase new products than their rural compatriots.

Shenzhen became an SEZ in the summer of 1980 together with the three other coastal cities of Zhuhai, Shantou, and Xiamen.[26] Shenzhen is known as the electronics manufacturing center in China, similar to Silicon Valley in the U.S. Its capitalistic economy, proximity to Hong Kong, and importance to the industry have made Shenzhen one of the most affluent cities in the Middle Kingdom. To date, Shenzhen has become a model for China's urban and economic growth. In 2003, the per capita disposable income for its city dwellers was 26,000 RMB ($3,150), almost 34 times what it was when it became an SEZ.[27] In addition to higher incomes, about seven out of ten Shenzhen households possess apartments or houses and one out of five households has title to its own automobile.

Teenagers in Shenzhen are automatically predisposed to better living conditions. A select few of the elite teenagers have parents who hold management positions at foreign companies that pay more than any domestic company. Shenzhen has better living conditions than those of other Mainland cities, and its close proximity to Hong Kong predisposes these privileged teens to better education, foods, and healthcare.

It is no wonder that Wal-Mart decided to set up its first Chinese Supercenter in Shenzhen.[28] Since the initial store opened in the summer of 1996, Shenzhen has blossomed into one of China's largest cities in terms of disposable income and other favorable demographics, all of which point toward a favorable youth market for many years to come.

Economic Trends

China's extraordinary growth, frequently heralded as the fastest in the world, is quickly turning it into an economic superpower. But China's case is much more significant compared to any other case, as its population is many times larger than most other developed countries.

China has the largest labor market in the world, which can explain why exports into China continue to soar from all regions of the world. Chinese exports to the United States reached $197 billion in 2004, doubling in just four years.[29] Further, China's growing infrastructure distinguishes it from other economic powers. In 2003, China consumed about 40 percent of the world's production of cement. In 2004, China surpassed Japan to become the world's second-largest importer of oil, after the U.S.[30] Although down from 9.5 percent in 2004, the country's GDP growth is still expected to be eight percent in 2005.[31]

The wealth generated in China, once relegated to the fringes of the country's eastern shores, can now be observed in the inland areas. Cities such as Nanchang in Jiangxi province and Wuhu in Auhui province were impoverished just a few years ago. But aggressive construction of streets and railways have made them key transport hubs between the flourishing deltas of the Pearl River and the Yangtze River.

Domestic consumption is increasing. According to Automotive Resources Asia, China sold 474,084 cars by April 2005, the most cars sold in Asia; yet car sales slowed in late 2004 because of loan regulations and gas prices, causing many to reevaluate their initial high growth estimates. China's rural economy, 800 million people strong, is becoming a more consumerist economy, though slower than the urban economy. Consumption of color televisions rose to 60 televisions per 100 rural households in 2001.[32] Mobile phones, electric fans, telephones, and motorbikes all had large jumps in rural consumption as well.

Gen Y is inheriting an optimistic future with its economy. Although it faces many problems, the economy is rapidly improving and growing. In just several years, the youth will take their economy to the next level, enlarging it to one of the world's greatest.

Notes

[1]"Foreign Investment in China." http://www.uschina.org/statistics/2005foreigninvestment.html.

[2]http://english.people.com.cn/200212/17/eng20021217_108629.shtml.

[3]Jun Jing, 2000, p. 18, French population 60 million. http://education.yahoo.com/reference/factbook/fr/popula.html.

[4]"Population Peak May Pose Grave Challenges." http://www.china.org.cn/english/Life/110210.htm.

[5]http://www.iiasa.ac.at/Research/LUC/ChinaFood/data/pop/pop_7.htm.

[6]http://www.census.gov/cgi-bin/ipc/idbagg.

[7]http://www.cpirc.org.cn/en/e5cendata1.htm.

[8]http://www.census.gov/ipc/www/idbpyr.html and type in piecemeal by slashes http://www.census.gov/cgi-bin/ipc/idbagg.

[9]http://mobiletechnews.com/info/2005/05/23/201556.html.

[10]http://www.newsgd.com/business/enterprise/200401170020.htm.

[11]http://news.morningstar.com/news/BW/M06/D09/20050609005098.html.

[12]http://seattletimes.nwsource.com/html/businesstechnology/2002324323_starbucks10.html.

[13]http://www.chinadaily.com.cn/english/doc/2004-03/25/content_317955.htm.

[14]http://www.china.org.cn/english/18309.htm.

[15]http://atn-riae.agr.ca/asia/e3292.htm and Jing 2000: 117 & 119.

[16]http://www.time.com/time/asia/features/china_cul_rev/advertising.html.

[17]Jun Jing, 2000, p. 104.

[18]http://sean.dougherty.org/econ/papers/EA_21.pdf.

[19]http://www.latimes.com/features/printedition/books/la-et-book22mar22,1,3547308.story?coll=la-headlines-bookreview&ctrack=2&cset=true.

[20]http://www.photius.com/countries/china/economy/china_economy_agriculture.html.

[21]http://www.chinadaily.com.cn/english/doc/2004-04/26/content_326356.htm and http://www.ilo.org/public/english/chinaforum/download/infonote2.pdf for 2002 levels.

[22]"The Next Long March." March 30, 2001. Vol. 27, No. 12. http://www.asiaweek.com/asiaweek/magazine/nations/ 0,8782,103420,00.html.

[23]http://www.friedlnet.com/images/free_chinese_statistical_ communique_2002.pdf. Table 13, p. 21.

[24]http://www.china.org.cn/baodao/english/newsandreport/ 2001feb/new3-3.htm.

[25]"New Consumption Trends for Children." Luo Zhongyun. http://www.bjreview.com.cn/200306/Business-200306(B).htm.

[26]http://www.businessweek.com/1999/99_36/c3645148.htm.

[27]http://www.bjreview.com.cn/200407/Business-200407(E).htm and http://english.people.com.cn/english/200008/30/eng20000830 _49331.html The latter's figures had to be adjusted to the former's more current figures.

[28]http://www.china.org.cn/english/BAT/38711.htm.

[29]http://usinfo.state.gov/eap/Archive/2005/Mar/03-517799.html.

[30]http://english.people.com.cn/200311/21eng20031121_128701. shtml.

[31]"Wen lowers 2005 economic growth target." By Liu Weiling. http://www.chinadaily.com.cn/english/doc/2005-03/06/ content_422130.htm.

[32]http://www.chinability.com/Durables.htm.

Chapter 8

Purchasing Power and Wants

This chapter will discuss the purchasing power and wants of the youth. Though much of the information may seem intended for business purposes, the youth's choices and wants are indicative of the vast changes occurring around them and indicate the reasoning for their decisions. The research in this chapter certainly reveals that the youth accept capitalistic ideals and Western products and, as a result of their country's transition from a planned to consumerist economy, now feel the need to be satisfied. Research points out the possibility of Chinese society, which has traditionally been a "we, communal society," becoming more of a "me and my family" society.

In a larger context, youth's choices also illustrate a larger problem concerning Chinese youth—confusion. Without guidance from experience, parents, or government, the youth have been infused with drastic changes and forced to make their own choices on their country's uncharted path to a modern country. None of the research shows that the youth conceptually tie their hard academic work to larger goals of building their economy—such as increasing market share or providing vast infrastructure. This alludes to a deficiency in the youth in regards to the ever-growing complexities of the global market, not taught in the strict, time-trusted Confucian models. Furthermore, if everything is given to them on a silver platter and they are devoid of goals other than making money for oneself and family, then the youth may not understand the global consequences of their decisions. The fact that this generation is devoid of experiences of war, devastation, and extreme poverty does not help such a deficiency. Both youth and marketers alike should be cognizant of these interesting choices and judge them in their own context.

Spending Money

China's Generation Y in urban areas differs from the adolescents of its parents' generation in having a far greater purchasing power. At school and on the streets, students have bigger and better toys that are rivaling those of their American and European counterparts. This surge in spending money is golden to marketers and sellers everywhere as they rush to peddle their wares to the product-thirsty youth. Though the amount spent may be slightly lower than that of American youth, the sheer number and eagerness of teens provides a wide market for sellers.

The major source of cash for Gen Y comes from its parents. Some of the youth do not have to earn allowances, ostensibly different from the lives of many American children. There is thus meaning in the nickname "little emperor/empress," indicating their tendency to be spoiled. One 1995 survey of 1,496 Beijing families ascertained that the single child in the family determined the allocation of nearly 70 percent of the family's expenditures. Given that there are more than 65 million families with an only child, Gen Y youth have great power to assert their will in family purchases.[1]

Gen Y teenagers can freely ask for more money should they run out, and their parents typically pay their mobile phone bills. This arrangement seems like a cash machine! One male declared that he will save the money from his parents to buy something he really wants. This statement, however, reflects an uncommon concept among the rest of the Chinese youth. It seems that these teens did not inherit a flair for saving from their parents.

Below is a sampling of how much the youth receive from their parents each month:

Younger Females	Older Females	Younger Males	Older Males
500-600	300-400	200	400
200	300	500	20 RMB/day
300-500		300	800
"When I run out of money, I can ask more from them, and they wouldn't limit how much I would use in a month." But usually 100-300.			"I have no idea. I will ask for more when I use it up."

Note: These figures include mobile phone bills.

Although throngs of teens may be flocking to stores, it should be mentioned that one of the games Gen Y teens play when shopping together is window-shopping. But teenagers will purchase more expensive items on their parents' money when they shop with them. With her parents' money, one female purchased a Siemens mobile phone, a watch, and jewelry, while her parents purchased a Sjtu Sunway computer, in spite of a monthly family income of 4,000 RMB. The pampering and sheltering of a generation is not beneficial for the youth and works to their disadvantage in development. China's obstacles in development require the youth to proceed with an economical mind-set. In addition, parental pampering provides insight into the apathies of some teens who have little idea of what they want to do for the rest of their lives. Also remember that members of Gen Y in wealthier families have the consolation of large inheritances because of the 4-2-1 family structure and money on demand. Modernization and development cannot occur with a generation that are parasites on their parents and grandparents.

Even more shocking is the realization that parents con-
sciously allow this to happen. How can parents hand over their
hard-earned money if they are as poor as the West portrays them
to be? The parents of Generation Y grew up during the rule of
Mao Zedong, who led the Cultural Revolution and made China
into a stalwart communistic nation. The young parents of Gen
Y struggled during these difficult years without any possessions
and constantly searching for their next meal. Unlike in America,
the families of the young parents saved every bit of money and,
consequently, China maintained the highest savings percentage
rate in the world.[2] However, in the past twenty years economic
growth has come to China, and the now-grown adults are determined to prevent their single children from experiencing the
same conditions they once endured. As a result, the parents have
the tendency to purchase high-ticket items for their beloved
single child, and will bequeath nearly half of their life savings to
him/her.

Boys generally received more money from their parents than
did girls. The reason for the income inequality may stem from
China's traditional inclination toward favoring males instead of
females. The one-child policy exacerbates this partiality because
traditionally the birth of a boy entailed more money for his family
and him. Moreover, in Chinese culture the male has a dominant
role in society. Although this preference is much more prevalent
in the rural areas of China, it is still present in many bustling
cities.

Working

**Now what do you think are the differences between
American and Chinese youth?**

Jiang: I think that American youth would like music; in terms
of lifestyle, I think they would be a bit more independent.
From a young age they start working, have part-time jobs,
and pay for school with their own money, I think.

The second major source of their income is working. West-ern fast-food chains provide the youth a purchasing power of around 400 RMB each month. One girl even dances to earn some extra money. However, the vast majority of teenagers noted that their parents are the sole source of their disposable income.

In large cities such as Beijing, Shanghai, Shenzhen, and Guangzhou parents usually do not make teenagers work if they do not have to because they want their children to focus on their ever-so- important grades. Working in high school does not pro-duce the same reverence in China as it does for teenagers in the United States. In fact, it can be said that some parents look down upon the thought of their children working. Parents believe that working and dating are major distractions from school, and will ultimately take away from their children's lives as well as from their own retirement.

This greatly differs from the American mind-set in which working is enthusiastically encouraged by college guidance coun-selors and parents. A huge milestone in an American's life is when he or she turns sixteen. One of the greatest advantages of turn-ing sixteen in America, besides driving, is the ability to work legally. Teenagers are finally able to earn their own money and spend it on whatever they wish. They can buy their own designer clothes and food. They exude a sense of responsibility and own-ership for the items they purchase, and they feel more indepen-dent from their parents—an important aspect of the American psyche.

This is not to say that all parents in China are against work-ing. In fact, the opposite view is held in poorer provinces, where children must work to support their parents who tend to the fields. However, if those living in rural areas had stronger eco-nomic means, it is highly probable that parents would ensure their children would focus on schooling.

Red Envelope Money

Another source of Gen Y's purchasing power is from Red Envelope or *hong bao* money. Red Envelope money is the money (in red envelopes) a child receives as a gift from parents, grandparents, and relatives during the Chinese New Year festivities. Red Envelopes are adorned with illustrations of Chinese calligraphy, symbolizing luck, joy, and riches. The gift of money is essentially a measure of love, as teenagers will receive more money from the close relatives in the family. Tradition has it that Gen Y can receive Red Envelopes with greater sums of cash for their weddings. The gift of money contrasts with the Western stigma against giving money as a present.

All teenagers mentioned they receive Red Envelope money, though the amounts differed. To some, it constitutes major buying power because the cash can be saved for when it is needed. Children who cannot wait will spend what they received after Chinese New Year, an especially profitable time for storekeepers.

Advertisements

In all areas of the world, marketers attempt to use celebrities to promote products in all media formats. The United States' market is unique, however. It is the one that has been inundated by advertisements since the days of radio. Advertising picked up momentum as television was invented and improved. Then movies, billboards, magazines, and newspapers all became major advertising sources. The United States, boasting its media hegemony over the globe, has developed distaste for its own celebrities' product endorsements. Often, Americans view actors and actresses who endorse products from corporations as sellouts. Artists such as Brad Pitt would never consider endorsing a product in the U.S. despite the potential to earn several million dollars in an hour's photo shoot. What most Americans do not know is that Pitt did advertisements for Tag Heuer, Rolex, Toyota, and numerous other corporations in Japan, Europe, and Latin America; especially in Japan, consumers flocked to the stores to purchase his endorsements. This anecdote illustrates the differences in the public's response to endorsements: America's Gen Y resents corporations' attempt to bond with them through their feeble attempts at understanding them.

The Chinese consumers are not different from their fellow Japanese consumers when it comes to effective advertising. In China, unlike in the States, young trendsetters flip through their Japanese magazines and television stations looking for celebrity endorsements; all teens unanimously agreed that they prefer celebrity endorsements. They are greatly influenced by those Chinese who have gained celebrity-like status in the United States and who endorse products on Chinese television.

Another example of successful celebrity endorsements in China is Pepsi. Known as *Bai Shi Ke Le* in China, Pepsi has capitalized the most on the youths' fascination with celebrities and has cast virtually all of them in its commercials. Illuminated Pepsi lanterns and billboards line the shopping district in Shanghai on Nanjing Road. One Pepsi commercial contained six local Chinese celebrities. Pepsi recently attempted a strong campaign of the same type of commercials in the States, including the likes of pop mega-diva Britney Spears, former senator Bob Dole, Ozzy Osbourne & family, and other lesser-known celebrities. Coke followed suit with Britney's rival, Christina Aguilera, thus making a dueling-divas competition. America's response to the duel can be expressed by a television show on E! in which commentators pleaded for the beverage makers to stop; America just could not handle it.

Sports television is a marketing strategy for Phillips Electronics. The company sponsored China's soccer team and subsequently has won the confidence as well as admiration of ten million students. Soccer is the most popular sport for university students in China. The company has marketed to the youth by establishing electronics fairs on university campuses and boasted $7.5 billion in profit from the Chinese market alone in 2003.[3]

Advertisements are everywhere in the large cities of China and indeed are necessary for youth living in a country that has only recently embraced consumerism and knows little about leisure products. An advertisement will be more efficacious if it is humorous and colorful. Nike attempts to be humorous in its advertisements in China. However, Nike learned a lesson in December 2004 when it aired an ad that the government found more culturally insensitive than humorous.[4] Consequently, the advertisement was pulled off the popular state-run sports television network. The commercial, *The Chamber of Fear*, showed American basketball star Lebron James fighting and winning against an ancient kung fu teacher.

Nike has a reputation for creating its own brand name and then molding it to make it "cool" in the eyes of the youth. Moreover, it makes its commercials humorous so that they joke with the viewer. Nike's brand reputation will continue to build upon itself in the future because it is greatly sought after by the youth and ostensibly the parents of the youth who buy their products.

What kind of advertisements will attract you to purchase games?

Cheng: Those with beautiful pictures.

Yang: As for the opening cartoon, 3D is better.

Jiang: ...Moreover, the public praising of the manufacturing company is quite important too.

Yang: I agree with him.

Sun: Me too.

Han: I have opinions similar to his.

—younger males

Generation Y wants to see advertisements that contain familiar celebrities or cartoons; moreover, male teenagers specifically want to see lots of colors and unique, contemporary packaging that is eye-catching and will spark their interest. An advertisement that contains sentiments showing a person as "cool," "trendy," and "Western" will spark interest with those who can afford such products. Advertisements should specifically show that the product empathizes with Gen Yers, deliver a message that the product will help children with their studies, make fun of the strict school environment, or make them feel that if they were to buy the product, all of their friends would be envious.

Reputation is critical to not only the youth, but also to adults. What goads the youth to buy expensive goods is the product's reputation. The same principle exists in the attitude toward universities and investing in the stock market. Prices are intensely driven by *mingqi* or reputation. Perceived reputation is often the best barometer for price fluctuations.[5] Just as stocks are driven by reputation, so too are college preferences among students. Products can build reputation just by their prices. Both parents and teenagers assume that expensive goods are of higher quality than cheaper ones and are willing to pay more for foreign goods if they expect that the product will last longer. Retailers should be delighted: a society that will gladly pay more if the product is of high quality and trendy!

One of the quintessential ad strategies is the one used by KFC to lure young Chinese into its stores. One of the reasons that KFC has been so successful (currently the largest fast-food chain in China) in marketing to the youth is because it has created a zany and colorful cartoon character called "Qiqi" that resembles the younger Colonel Sanders dressed in hip-hop clothing, and a slogan that reads, "Study hard, play hard" (*renzhen xuexi, kaixin youxi*).[6] KFC noticed that youth could not relate to the original Colonel Sanders character, and decided to scrap it. Ultimately, the chain's success hinges on its accomplishment in making the restaurant domestic and a part of adolescence for Generation Y, making its hordes of patrons lifelong customers.[7]

Other corporations directly target the youth through advertising. H.J. Heinz developed a strategy that targeted university students in large cities who would adopt the brand and cause other individuals to follow.[8] Heinz created television commercials that boasted healthy ingredients in cereal and displayed its foreign name, which persuaded some consumers that the product was healthier than domestic substitutes.[47]

One of the emerging trends in advertisements in China is product endorsement by local Chinese celebrities. The best example of this trend's success is Yao Ming, the 7'5"-tall basketball star of the Houston Rockets. Born and raised in Shanghai, Yao was the first pick in the National Basketball Association draft in 2002 and is now a household name in China and the U.S. When Yao traveled to China to play preseason NBA games in Shanghai and Beijing in 2004, nearly 200 million Chinese people watched them. He has been the target of many billion-dollar companies' pleas for his endorsement of their products. In 2004, McDonald's inked a multiyear global partnership with the Chinese celebrity. McDonald's executives are elated at the performance of Yao Ming and have even deemed him "the first-ever worldwide brand ambassador." Reebok has seen its profits rising nearly $200 million. Pepsi says its profits have risen nearly 30 percent after Yao Ming's endorsements under the slogan "Dare for More," and is planning to launch Gatorade in China through Yao's endorsements.

Yao Ming has been seen in several American commercials, including Apple's G4 Powerbook and Visa's Superbowl ads. Media giant Disney is trying to get Yao to help establish its brand name in China as it opens its first park in Hong Kong in 2006 and launches its famous show "the Wonderful World of Disney" on Chinese television. China Unicom and Sohu.com, a popular site for the youth in Internet Gaming, are promoting fan websites about him on the Internet in tandem with an American firm. Yao Ming can definitely enjoy his fat salary, which has risen 300 percent since he played in the U.S., but he must give nearly 33 percent to the central government in Beijing, a stipulation for permission to play in America. Already corporate scouts are at Yao's games, trying to get the star to endorse their products at the 2008 Beijing Olympics.

Porsches, Ferraris, Lamborghinis, Oh My!

Though China currently does not have a pervasive brand culture, brand recognition is certainly growing, primarily among the youth. Gen Y is especially vulnerable to Internet brand advertising, which has the ability to instill a company's name, slogan, or image in a computer gamer who stares at the screen for hours each day. The importance of brands can be seen on wish lists in which several teens desired Ferraris and Lamborghinis, two brands that only very recently entered a market in which relatively few people can purchase their products. Because the brands are so new, it is the youth, and not their parents, who are knowledgeable about them.

What cars do you want to buy when you grow up?
Jiang: Mercedes-Benz
Yang: Benz
Sun: Ferrari
Qin: BMW
Han: Peugeot, from France
Cheng: Lincoln

—younger males

Moreover, in the urban areas there is a slight feeling of competition among teenagers: to show how much money or popularity one has. Gen Y is choosing brands because of advertisements and its lifestyle. My home-stay brother purchased $100 Nike shoes because of its advertisements and brand reputation.

179

One teen wants a Jeep because she is very athletic and Jeep fits her lifestyle. Others are interested in showing off their new toys to their friends. At the school lunch table teenagers congregate to flaunt the brand names of their new technological gadgets and clothing, easily keeping up with their friends.

Females are most heavily influenced by Western ways and brands, knowing exactly which brands are in style from their purchases of Japanese trend magazines. They have been influenced by fashion-forward Westernized trends that range from Gap and Gucci to Victoria's Secret and Fendi, and buy athletic clothes from Nike, Umbro, and Adidas. As modern females, they are familiar with Avon, Clinique, Lancome, L'Oreal, and other leading cosmetics brands, purchasing them whenever they can. Their cell phones, which could cost around 2,000 RMB ($250), must be small, fashionable, and be Web-enabled to give them the ability to download games and music via the Internet. Males prefer to buy Nike, Adidas, Sony, and Samsung branded products.

Current and Past Purchases

A key barometer for the growing purchasing power of teenagers in China is the growth in nonfood sales over the past few years, which increased 13.2 percent in 2004 from sales in the same month the previous year.[9] During that year, retail sales in rural areas grew 10.7 percent, while retail sales grew 14.5 percent in urban areas.

Marketers should be optimistic: as the focus groups indicate, all younger females and at least three-fourths of the eight older girls remarked that they had a high propensity to purchase telecommunications, consumer electronics, and cosmetic products in two to three years. Their thirst for cosmetics is indicative of the Chinese cosmetics market, which currently is the eighth largest in the world, growing at 10 percent each year.[10] Mary Kay launched an upscale "Timewise" cosmetics line aimed at young females and young white-collar females. Mary Kay, which entered the Chinese market in 1998 and had to do away with its direct-selling model to suit the China market, is going gangbusters with annual sales that were reportedly close to one billion RMB in 2002. [11]

As China becomes more economically developed and modernized, a strong increase in the youth's purchasing power of Western items is to be expected. Generation Y is and will continue to benefit from its parents' increased earnings. Those earnings, attributed to new jobs created by foreign capital and a freer market economy, will be greatly enhanced at the time when Gen Yers enter the workforce and help transform the Chinese economy into a consumer economy.

The lives of the "little emperors" are filled with state-of-the-art technology at a level unknown in the United States. Younger or older, all of the Chinese teenagers spend at least some part of their money on electronics, either for gaming or cell phones. The teenagers are very educated when it comes to consumer electronics, as they have recently purchased PCs, MP3 players, CDs, and CD-based software. Other recently purchased items include cell phones from Motorola, Alcatel, and Siemens; Hewlett Packard printers; and Nike sneakers. They tend to purchase low-end items (e.g., apparel and CDs) on their own, but electronics and other higher-end products such as bicycles and watches are typically purchased with the help of parents. Generation Y of Shanghai primarily purchases cell phones and other products at specialty outlets for electronics and at department stores such as the Oriental Department Store in Shanghai and Dimei Mall.

Some male teens are captivated by gaming toys like Pokémon action figures. One 18-year-old male happily demonstrated his action figure key chain, on which he put all of his keys. Herein is a difference between the American Generation Y and the Chinese Generation Y. Unlike in China, electronic gaming is not nearly as popular for teenagers in the United States; and likewise, students would not usually carry gaming paraphernalia. If a teenager attending an ordinary school in the United States were to sport a computer game action figure in any way, he in all probability would be ostracized and ridiculed; worse, he would be placed in a lower caste in the school social hierarchy—a dreadful result for many insecure teenagers.

Unlike the girls, boys are rather rebellious when purchasing items with which their parents do not agree. The boys will purchase the goods anyway and negotiate with their parents later. The males claim that parents only want to pay for "conventional" items, not coveted model airplanes and video games. As a result, older boys purchase products on their own initiative that their parents do not want them to buy, going to Shanghai's Nanjing Road and Xujiahui Road (pronounced "Shoo Ja Hway"), both wide boulevards with large department stores.

With their allowances that range from 100 RMB to 600 RMB ($12-75) per month, the younger teenage girls can be considered heavy purchasers of personal care products, such as makeup and hair care items. Parents tend to purchase higher ticket items (electronics and necessities) than their daughters and tend to influence purchasing decisions for products and services over 200 RMB ($25). Even with allowances, the teens often ask for, and receive, additional money from their parents (upward of 400 RMB or $50 a month), which gives them even greater purchasing power. All told, the products they tend to buy on their own comprise apparel (shoulder bags and wallets), footwear (Nike tennis shoes), CDs, books, and cosmetics (Up2U—owned by Avon Cosmetics). The younger females also purchase their own clothing and concert tickets because the parents do not share their teenagers' taste in these items.

What Would You Buy for $125?

Perhaps the greatest indication of the vast changes occurring in Chinese cities was the response of am 18-year-old when I asked him what he would buy for $125. He chuckled and responded, "You can't buy anything for $125 these days."

If young teenage girls were given 1,000 RMB ($125), they would purchase apparel, food, perfume, lingerie, cosmetics, portable electronics, CDs, software, and other forms of computer-based entertainment.

If you are given 1,000 RMB, what will you buy?

Yang: A Sony digital camera.

Wang J.: How can you buy it with 1,000?

Yang: Second-hand. Even a second-hand one is better than a national brand.

Xu W.: Game software and machine. Chinese ones are okay. Japanese and Korean ones are also okay.

Wang J.: I will buy small computer parts with 1,000 RMB. I will change the mouse and keyboard and add an anti-dust protection.

Wang X.: I will buy some attachments for my devices and some CDs and tapes...I mean my electronics at home. I will buy them from Japan.

Lu: CDs and shoes. No special CD type.

Zhan: I will take it as pocket money and buy something to eat.

Wu: I will buy household electronics and a Sony camera.

Xu J.: I will save it; I don't know what to buy.

Older girls want to purchase items of their own will and would not listen to their parents when it comes to shopping. The 17- to 18-year-olds place a greater emphasis on their vanity, as they mentioned makeup, hair dye, apparel, footwear, CDs, software, and food—presumably Americanized fast food and casual restaurant brands.

Recently purchased brands have included Za foundation makeup, Etam skirts, and Daphne sneakers. Higher-ticket items have included a Samsung flat screen TV, a Giant bicycle, and a Lenovo (Legend) computer. As for preferred brand names, the group cited Nokia and Motorola as perhaps the dominant cell phone brands and consumer electronics from Sony. While they surely influence such purchase decisions, their parents typically purchase such products at hypermarkets like Carrefour and department stores. The teens themselves prefer to shop on Xiangyang Road for knockoffs, Xujiahui Area, and other large department stores.

Future Purchases

The future of Gen Y around the world is filled with hopes of expensive products, such as the biggest house and the most powerful car. China's intense modernization and advertisements have inculcated the ambitious need to be satisfied —one of the rudiments of consumerism. China's youth envision a future with more opulent estates, fancy cars, high-tech electronics, plasma television, and advanced computer software. As long as the reputation of foreign goods is superior to that of domestic, China's youth prefer and will pay more for foreign goods. This aura of consumer spirit should give both marketers and foreign companies reason for optimism.

Younger Girls

The younger females are especially positive about buying foreign goods. They hope to purchase cell phones made in Japan, notebooks, blue jeans, and cars from the U.S. manufacturers, electronics from Japan and Germany, and European designer apparel. Although they mentioned cars, most of the young girls did not see themselves driving cars—they want to be driven. Half expect to purchase a house in Shanghai, and, similar to their older female peers, want to buy houses and cars for their parents. Young girls also carry mobile phones but find it burdensome that parents can easily find them and their charges; as a result they look for mobile phones that can screen their calls, are small in size, and have varied colored faceplates.

The following lists some of the products that each said she would like to purchase over the next decade:

Zhou: European car, high-end digital electronics, and a house.

Zhang S.: BMW, notebook computer, Dolce & Gabana perfume, and a mobile phone.

Tao: A house, a notebook computer, and an electronic dog from Japan.

Zhang Y.: A house, a car, and a robot.

Jiang: European car, digital products, a house, and a housecleaner.

Xu: Perfume from Paris, Japanese-designed house, South African diamonds, and candy from Belgium.

Yao: High-end mobile phone, laptop, and digital camera.

Ni: Mobile phone, American apparel, and a digital camera from Japan.

Gen Yers crave Japan's more advanced technology, judging Japanese electronics to be far superior to American. Several of the Chinese youth even want to purchase robots from Japanese companies in the future; depending on fate, Generation Y will probably be the first generation in China to see and be receptive to such a marvel. The teens' reception to modernization is an important concept, as it illustrates the character and peculiarities of this new generation. Their fascination with technology and proximity to Japan may make China a competing producer of electronics in the future.

Older Girls

Looking into other possible future product purchases, the 17-
to 19-year-old teens identified brands and products that they
would likely purchase within the next decade. These included
PCs from the United States (IBM), cosmetics from Europe
(Lancôme), and electronics from Korea and Japan, as summarized below. They also anticipate buying nice clothes, a robot,
and a house. Some older girls see themselves purchasing cars in
the next ten years, specifically German cars such as BMWs and
Porsches, and other expensive cars like Bentley and Rolls Royce,
which range in price from $212,000 to $356,000 in China.[12]

> Zhu: Sony mobile phone, car from Germany, house, ste-
> reo, imported clothes, a Jay Zhou concert.
>
> Ye: German car, Clinique cosmetics, and Etam clothes.
>
> Wang: Electronic pet, car from Japan or South Korea, Vidi-
> con, videophone, and to meet Jay Zhou in person.
>
> Gao: A Jeep, computer, house, and dog.
>
> Wang L.: A car and a robot pet from Japan.
>
> Qiu: A BMW and apparel from France (Channel) and Italy
> (Armani).
>
> Zhang: Cell phone, Lancôme cosmetics, IBM PC, and a
> Porsche.
>
> Huang: A BMW, a Samsung HDTV, a Sony Vidicon cam-
> era, and a dog.

Finally, the group had various wants on its wish list if it
were given $125 to spend. Most of the items the older females
would purchase centered on their appearance and entertainment
needs. One would spend money to straighten her hair, and another would stock up on color cosmetics. Several mentioned
they would purchase clothes, and one mentioned she would buy
apparel from Igor. Two teens answered that they would buy food

either to make themselves healthier or give some to their parents.

The females hope to purchase homes and cars for their parents in the future. Though some of the preferences may not be realistic, the extravagance of females' wishes illustrates the importance of family and the potential for Gen Y to purchase gifts for their family. American parents must be so jealous!

Older Boys

The older boys are frequent users of cell phones. Seven of the eight have their own cell phones, and all said that at least one member of their household has a mobile phone. If they were in the market for a cell phone, they would pay between $250 and $375, and certainly would want it to be packed with state-of-the-art features.

Similar to the other teenage groups, their future purchases over the next decade starkly contrast with current purchases. The brands of vehicles they mentioned were predominately BMW, though one cited Toyota. Other items were Japanese electronics, computers, and other digital products. Interestingly, one noted that he plans to purchase a Spanish-style villa and a "big dog" as a pet. The following lists some of the products that each of the younger boys said he would like to purchase over the next decade:

Xu: BMW, a house, and an Apple computer.

Wu: Toyota car, Toshiba laptop, a big dog, and a villa.

Zhan: A BMW.

Lu: Japanese electronics and a European or American car.

Wang X.: Digital electronics from Sony, NEC, Panasonic, Toshiba, and Kenwood.

Wang J.: A house and a car.

Xu: Mobile phone and a computer from America.

Yang: Mobile phone and a computer.

Younger Boys

Similar to older males, cell phone ownership and usage have become as ubiquitous and pervasive in the young boys' lives as have computer games. Seven of the eight have their own cell phones. If they were going to purchase a new mobile phone as they often do, the teenagers would be willing to spend between 2,000 to 5,000 RMB ($250-625). As for features and looks, the group responded with a fairly homogenous list: digital cameras with high resolution, MP3 capabilities, downloading picture capabilities, varied ringing tones, and more masculine colors such as black, silver, or gray. The following lists some of the products that each said he would like to purchase over the next decade:

Cheng: Electronics, computers, and mobile phones.

Zhu: Sony PlayStation or Xbox.

Jiang: Computers, computer games, and apparel.

Xu: Computer games (PlayStation).

Han: Japanese electronics and American furniture.

Yang: Apparel and electronics from Japan and South Korea.

Sun: PlayStation 2, MP3 player, Polo shirts from Ralph Lauren.

Qin: Electronics from Japan and America and apparel from Italy.

The male teens expect to purchase apparel from Italy, electronics from Korea and Japan, cell phones and PCs from the United States, and fast food from American quick-service chains like McDonald's and KFC. Some of the vehicles they mentioned were Mercedes, Ferrari, BMW, Peugeot, and Lincoln.

The wish lists illustrate the optimism that the youth have about their future and economy. Though most of the youth understand they will not be able to drive a Ferrari, it remains a question as to how many of the youth have endless optimism after looking at hundreds of cranes building skyscrapers every day.

Domestic vs. International Brands

Nearly all of the groups preferred international brands to domestic brands. The teenagers were asked, "If Chinese brands were to improve, would you still purchase foreign products?" Most said that they would still buy foreign, though some mentioned that they would purchase domestic because of price considerations. They determined how much they believed a product from a particular region should cost if the product were offered at 10 RMB, a little more than a dollar. The results from this question were strikingly similar for all groups. A brand's reputation and perceived quality are the most important factors in their decision to buy an expensive gift.

Younger Girls

The following table outlines the younger girls' responses when it comes to choosing between domestic and international brands

Product	Domestic Brand	International Brand	Unsure
Sneakers/Footwear	0	8	0
Restaurant	5	3	0
Clothing	0	8	0
Cellular phone	0	8	0
Automotives	0	8	0
Food	6	2	0
Personal care items	0	8	0
Pharmaceutical/Drugs	7	1	0
Electronics	0	8	0
Financial services/Banking	3	5	0
Other	0	0	0

for many product categories. Clearly, the younger teenage girls prefer international brands to domestic ones. As one female put it simply: "The better reputation the brand has, the higher quality the product."

For product preferences, the younger females conveyed positive attitudes toward Japanese electronics from Sony and Panasonic. They favor European brands such as IKEA furniture, cosmetics and fragrances from Christian Dior and Chanel, European cars, and imported clothing. Five of the eight girls expressed positive sentiments toward Western-style stores in China (e.g., Carrefour), while the other three were neutral.

Older Girls

The older girls' responses are summarized in the following table segmented by domestic vs. international brands for various product categories.

All eight older girls preferred international brands to domestic ones when it came to personal care products. Some of the brands they mentioned included Vichy, Yayao, Arche, Shiseido (Japan), Za, and Olay (Procter & Gamble). Similar sen-

Product	Domestic Brand	International Brand	Unsure
Fast food	0	8	0
Sneakers/Footwear	0	8	0
Restaurant	1	7	0
Clothing	1	7	0
Cellular phone	1	7	0
Automotives	0	8	0
Food	2	4	2
Personal care items	1	7	0
Pharmaceutical/Drugs	7	1	0
Electronics	0	8	0
Financial services/Banking	5	3	0
Other	0	0	0

timents for international brands were a conveyed for electronics, as they mentioned several leading brands (Sony, Panasonic, and Samsung). The group, however, said they preferred domestic brands when it came to healthcare products and financial services. Overall, six of the eight older girls said they support choosing foreign brands.

As for brand preferences, the names mentioned were quite similar to the younger teenage group of females. They included Starbucks and KFC, Adidas and Nike footwear, Japanese steakhouses, Nokia, Siemens, and Erickson phones, BMW and Ferrari cars, Shiseido and Clinique cosmetics, and Sony and Samsung electronics. Their rationale for the vast preference of international brands was that they are more expensive and thus more durable.

Younger Boys

The following table outlines the younger boys' preferences for domestic vs. international brands across a number of different product categories.

Product	Domestic Brand	International Brand	Unsure
Fast Food	1	7	0
Sneakers/Footwear	1	7	0
Restaurant	3	0	5
Clothing	1	2	5
Cellular phone	0	8	0
Automotives	0	8	0
Food	2	1	5
Personal care items	0	0	8
Pharmaceutical/Drugs	1	2	5
Electronics	1	5	2
Financial services/Banking	1	2	5
Other	0	0	0

Clearly, they are quality-conscious and thus not very loyal to local brands. Seven of eight younger boys want to wear Nike and other imported footwear, and prefer international brands for automobiles, cell phones, and other electronics. Unlike the female groups, virtually none conveyed brand preferences when it came to food, personal care items, banking, and healthcare brands. The one consistent philosophy generated from their opinions was that they do not care where the products are produced, as long as they are high in quality. As such, they would purchase either domestic or international brands based on their own decisions and quality quotients, especially when it comes to apparel. The one disparity of those sentiments pertained to their retailer preferences. The teens said they prefer domestic retail stores. This could indicate that they are not very loyal to American merchants that have opened stores throughout China, such as Wal-Mart and Carrefour.

Older Boys
This contingent also has a preference for Western and international brands, such as American apparel, McDonald's, KFC, Pizza Hut, Nike, European watches (Swatch), and Reebok. Other international brands mentioned included German and Italian automobiles from the likes of BMW, Volkswagen, and Ferrari, Kao personal care items, and Toshiba electronics from Japan. The following table summarizes their preferences between domestic and international brands.

The brand preferences are not necessarily the same for their parents, who are not as brand-conscious. Yet half of the older boys said their parents support and exert strong influence over the purchase of foreign products. As for their attitudes toward certain industries, the group provided positive responses for high-tech industries (electronics and telecommunications) along with the apparel and retail sectors, and were either neutral or negative on healthcare industries. Half favors traditional Chinese medications, while the other half prefers Western-style pharmaceuticals.

192

Product	Domestic Brand	International Brand	Unsure
Fast Food	0	8	0
Sneakers/Footwear	0	8	0
Restaurant	2	4	2
Clothing	0	8	0
Cellular phone	0	8	0
Automotives	0	8	0
Food	4	3	1
Personal care items	1	7	0
Pharmaceutical/Drugs	4	4	0
Electronics	0	8	0
Financial services/Banking	4	4	0
Other	0	0	0

Based on Chinese youths' current purchases, future purchases, and preference for international brands, the United States clearly has a huge market potential in selling to Chinese consumers. The youth believe Chinese products are poor in quality. It is often this reputation of American and European goods as being higher in quality that makes teenagers purchase them—and at a higher price. Their parents have an important, although not final, say in the teens' decisions, and wooing parents is a perfect means to increasing sales. Appealing to the youths' purchasing habits is the best means to build a brand reputation with them.

Brand choices and wish lists are indicative of the nascent consumerist culture. The youth sounded as brand conscious as their counterparts in the States or Japan. On a grander scale, this consciousness emphasizes the intense changes, both social and economic, that are pervading China. Consumerism procures cosmopolitanism and choice—crucial elements of the global economy of which China's Gen Y seeks to be a part. But the wave of change is primarily hitting the nation's east coast, leaving rural Gen Y in the dark.

Notes

[1]Jun Jing, 2000, p. 6, p. 68.

[2]AsianInsight.com.

[3]http://en.ce.cn/main/Industries/200407/01/t20040701_1165495.
shtml.

[4]http://www2.chinadaily.com.cn/english/doc/2004-12/22/
content_402383.htm.

[5]Suzanne Gottschang and Lyn Jeffery, p. 283.

[6]Jun Jing, 2000, p. 119.

[7]Jun Jing, 2000, p. 134.

[8]Jun Jing, 2000, p. 19.

[9]http://www.chinaembassy.org.in/eng/zgbd/t147285.htm

[10]http://strategis.ic.gc.ca/epic/Internet/inimr-ri.nsf/en/gr109991e.
html.

[11]http://www.chinatoday.com.cn/English/e2004/e200404/p18.htm.
Also timewise source.

[12]http://english.people.com.cn/english/200105/11/eng20010511
_69673.html.

Chapter 9

A Promising Future

C hina is a closed community of 1.3 billion people, a world in which societal morals and tradition dictate life; "we" do an activity, not "I." Generation Y is no exception, although they live in an economy with one of the fastest growth rates that will increase its purchasing power and socioeconomic relations for many years to come.

Life through the Eyes of China's Gen Y

From childhood the youth are doted upon as the sole bearers of the proud family name, sharing not with siblings but with parents and grandparents. Life is not about self, but about obeying elders, state, and employers for the greater good. They must sacrifice money, happiness, creativity, and freedom for the community. They are supervised by the government as well as by their parents and grandparents; and in many cases business is not conducted by contracts, but by relationships and verbal agreements.

The youth are part of a country with a proud history that rivals the successes of most ancient civilizations, and includes fifty tumultuous years of the recent past. Currently living in a stable environment, the children are able to enjoy possibilities their parents could never imagine. They no longer feel hunger or fear death. They have only seen peace and stability and have basked in the higher earnings of their parents, creating an air of optimism never experienced by their parents who had been ravaged by famine and political insecurity. Contradicting that country's history, traditions, and culture, Western culture emphasizes freedom, individualism at the expense of the community, openness and vulgarity, less support in difficult times, and loneliness. Chinese proverbs clash with advertisements; consumerism clashes with Maoist doctrine. In contrast to what Chinese education theories propose, there is no model for the youth to follow; they must choose their paths by themselves. With capitalism's ostensible advantages for China, a whole wave of new problems has come with it.

Though Chinese culture has been inculcated into the youth, they widely participate in a laundry list of the Western decadences Mao fought to expel. The resulting generation gap is not only predicated on the differences in times, but also by the differences between the two adverse ideologies. Both ideologies snipe at each other, and Gen Y is stuck in the cross fire.

Capitalism and consumerism have always been part of the battle. All people in China have benefited from capitalism, though the extent has varied considerably. However, the ideological warfare is yet to be determined. Gender equality, the amount of individualism, and the importance of self-pleasure are all variables in China's future culture. What will emerge is a modern culture that stresses the importance of the communal obligations yet incorporates the individual, bridging the gaps between the two ideologies. Unbeknownst to some teenagers, their role is to set the tone of China's modern culture through their thoughts and decisions.

My Life As a Chinese Teenager

I would like to think that my journey to China was similar to the journey an average teenager of China's Gen Y is undergoing right now: an optimistic and enthusiastic journey in a new world experienced by an ambitious teenager.

196

To research China's Generation Y teenagers, I went to China and lived in a lower-middle-class neighborhood in northern Shanghai from July through September 2004. During my visits to China, I, similar to Chinese teenagers, was immersed in a new and changing world. Living with the Zhengs, a typical Chinese family in Shanghai, gave me true insight into the daily lives of China's Gen Y unnoticed by Western news magazines that publish articles on China every week. Mr. and Mrs. Zheng, Tim (a Gen Y singleton age15), and I essentially became a family.

To be fully immersed I ate Chinese food every day like a Chinese teen. Mrs. Zheng was a wonderful cook who spent three to four hours every night painstakingly preparing meals for her husband and son. She was very in tune with tradition, as she was a teacher at a demanding school. Some afternoons she would walk to a nearby alleyway where she purchased a chicken that was killed just before she brought it home. She would complement the chicken with rice, vegetables, and soup. I soon learned that I would not be drinking Coke because the Chinese usually use soup to wash down their food. On some mornings she would serve dumplings and Wonton soup that she made herself, not packaged or purchased from a supermarket. One morning we went into a back alleyway, a thoroughfare of people walking and biking. Tim took me to—there is no other way to describe it—a decrepit shack, eight by eight feet with nothing more than a picnic table inside (not even a cash register), in which we ate noodles for breakfast. The owner of the restaurant made the noodles himself by shaping the dough and cooking it in stew.

Amidst all the Western development and cultural influences like KFC and McDonald's, I was surprised to learn that the Zhengs, similar to most Chinese people, have a very vague understanding of Western food, except that it consists of McDonald's and KFC. Unlike in the U.S., Chinese cities do not yet have an international cuisine because the country has been closed off for half a century. KFC had blended in so well with Chinese culture that Tim had the vague notion that he was taking me to a local restaurant. One day we even went to a Mexican restaurant in Shanghai, marking the first time that Tim and his mother used a knife and fork.

The extent to which KFC has saturated China and its youth is truly impressive. I kept thinking that the British attempted to sell products to the Chinese at the turn of the twentieth century but could only get them addicted to opium, yet KFC has so easily addicted China's Generation Y. Even if the youth do not eat at KFC, they still hear about their friends working there. Restaurants are youthful, energetic, and "cool," shoving both chicken and pop culture down their throats. McDonald's restaurants have strategically placed arcades adjacent to or connected to them.

Mrs. Zheng was always very accommodating, and her attention to me was most likely a result of either my being a guest or being seen as a child. It appears the latter is more accurate, for everywhere I went I was treated like a child, in spite of my adult-like project of writing this book. She believed I would be lonely at night and often checked up on me to ensure that I was okay. Furthermore, the Zhengs took me to a dinner banquet one night with all of Mrs. Zheng's coworkers who helped tutor Tim for his secondary entrance exams at his prestigious language school. I sat adjacent to an elderly English teacher whose English was very difficult to understand. At one point she mentioned that I was silent and "timid like a girl." I thereby realized traditional values and qualities are very important to older generations. I tend to believe that despite slight changes in values and traditions, these ideas of seniority will remain intact, as teenagers accept ancient filial roles and Confucian values.

Tim was spoiled. He had access to his personal computer, the Internet, and a car costing 40,000 RMB. Every night after finishing dinner Mrs. Zheng would tell her son and me to rest in the living room while she cleaned up the dishes. She would not even hear of me trying to help her. The major task of the child was to maintain his outstanding grades at school and succeed at his entrance exams. The teenagers like Tim are thus fully "dependent" on their families for financial support. Tim was proud of his $100 Nike shoes and expensive Adidas sweatpants, and his mother was glad to see him wear them. Mrs. Zheng was just introduced to the consumer culture in Shanghai and was still learning the procedures of shopping in the department stores to which her son had more exposure. She could hardly believe the changes of the times. When we went to the Shanghai exposition and saw a replica of Shanghai in the 1930s, Mrs. Zheng looked like a nostalgic, proud child in a candy store.

Tim and I decided one night to go swimming in the local pool. The enormous pool, an oasis of recreation in an urban jungle, was crowded into the middle of canyons of high-rises. The nurse who performed a brief physical required for swimming smiled broadly as I lifted the hat I was wearing. Tim mentioned later that I was the first Westerner she had seen with such light hair. Literally hundreds of people were swimming in the pool, leaving so little space that I tacitly questioned Tim's attraction to such a busy pool. My hair frequently caught the attention of the young swimmers. It was a group of teenagers who catalyzed a conversation with me, all of us talking about life and asking questions about each other's cultures while freezing in the cool water. One male's optimism in regard to the university he would attend exemplifies the optimism of Gen Y. He wanted me to know that the Chinese youth were catching up with the West in both living conditions and intelligence. Leaving the pool, we watched the surroundings where we encountered another clique of teenage males playing basketball; on seeing me leaving the pool they chuckled *waiguoren* (foreigner).

Although he was not obsessed with playing video games, Tim showed me his favorite. The freedom he had in playing and choosing the setting contrasted so much with his life. A product of the robotic Chinese education system, Tim was especially quiet and submissive due to his superior academic aptitude. When we played his math card game, invented by his mother's friends, he took the game quite seriously and I lost—badly; I lost face in that round. He was held tightly in his parents' lifestyle, shut out from the world, and immature for his age compared to American teens, spending time with his parents on the weekends so as not to be diverted from his grades and exam study time.

Though Tim would never say that we came into conflict, we did. Tim was quite uncomfortable later during my stay. Partially fueling his discontentment was the fact that, originally unbeknownst to me, he relinquished his room to me. His parents were doting on me because I became the new little emperor. Moreover, Mr. and Mrs. Zheng constantly told Tim "to be more like Michael." At one point, Mr. Zheng mentioned that his son's voice was high for his age, making Tim feel embarrassed. In response, Tim either quietly shook his head or smiled as he lost face, because people in the Chinese culture are taught not to show anger or embarrassment in front of others.

My coming had inadvertently taken away his belongings, his dignity, and his parents, essentially upsetting his life as an only child unlike no other peer had previously done. Chinese parents generally are more honest and critical of their children than American parents, who will take the side of their children when they shouldn't and lie in order to make their children feel better. Mrs. Zheng's occupation as a teacher predisposed her to being strict with her son. Her husband's and her behavior should not be viewed as a means to hurt their child, but quite the opposite—to push their son to succeed at a significant period in his life. Their academic standards and ploys were successful enough that their son attended one of the most prestigious schools in Shanghai.

It is not Chinese custom to be aggressive—at least on the outside—and as a rule, the general population of China adheres to it. The differences in cultural perception of aggression are illustrated in the workplace, where Americans generally excel more quickly than their Chinese coworkers who, although equally or more qualified, are modest and not as self-promoting as their American coworkers.

The Zhengs believed that I was there by fate, a common belief, and would have a large impact on their child. Chinese children are heavily swayed by friends, acquaintances, and parents. Confucian belief holds that the people one meets in life are role models. For instance, one teen stated that she wanted to travel to Tibet because her teacher had been there and showed pictures to the class. The belief implies that everybody one meets is fated to be there. It explains the youth's dependence and propensity to follow others, contradicting the American belief that "I am my own soldier," proclaimed dramatically in American Army commercials. Parents in America assert this ideal to discourage their child from following other influences. Most American children grow up hearing the perennial admonishment used by parents, "Would you jump off of a bridge if your friends did?"

In Shanghai, the communal atmosphere is highly palpable at night, when the noises of people talking, yelling, and laughing penetrate thin walls. Listening to the sounds at night from my room, I could hear and see fireworks being shot off unsafely from the narrow alleyways between high-rises; fireworks were often used to celebrate with others when moving into new houses and other special celebrations. In addition, in Beijing I heard the drunken singing of old communist songs connoting a feeling of community. This ambience and my relations with my home-stay family made me feel welcome in Chinese society.

My taxi experiences in Shanghai were truly unforgettable. Finding a taxi during morning rush hour is a battle, one that I often lost due to the sheer volume of people who take taxis in the morning—including many teenagers. Taxis are very inexpensive, costing approximately 22 RMB ($2.65) to go about a mile. One day I spent half an hour trying to find a cab to take me to Nanjing Road in Shanghai, but to no avail. Mrs. Zheng then hailed down a moped rider who would take me to my destination for ten RMB—a dollar. It was then that I realized how dangerous the driving was in China, and I henceforth remained on four wheels.

Though the education system has given China a high literacy rate and has made China more competitive in the global market, it takes its toll on the personalities of people. A couple of teenagers had trouble expressing who they really were. Jiang Q. muttered, "I'm not extraordinary. I just study." And coupled with parental shielding, it prevents the youth from thinking creatively. Part of the reason for China's piracy is its people's proclivity to imitating, instead of innovating and inventing, Western and Japanese goods and techniques. As a result of the lack of creativity, fads have an extra impact in China if the youth can relate to them.

Perhaps the most suspenseful event during my life as a Chinese teenager occurred in Beijing when my pocket was picked while in a shopping center buying counterfeit luggage and DVDs. As I made my way to the police station and declared the crime, I realized that it would be no use. However, if caught, the thief would receive a strict penalty, as crimes against foreigners are held especially heinous in China. The chief officer highlighted the differences between Western and Chinese youth by commending me, a teenager, on traveling to Beijing alone. As he put it, "Chinese parents would never let their children go alone to another country."

The picture painted throughout this book has been very optimistic about the future for China's Generation Y, but it is easy to get lost in the glitter of China's business world and lose sight of reality. Western businesspeople may be so captivated by the conspicuously beautiful highways leading from the international airports and the tall buildings and high-speed trains that they paint a rosy picture of the rapid growth of the Chinese nation to superpower status. The reality is that China still faces many obstacles in its path to become a superpower. Chief among them is the lack of a sound and powerful legal system; the current structure is laden with loopholes and corrupt judges. More laws are being created through precedents now, but the system has a long way to go to reach the Western standard. Chinese businesses base their endeavors and decisions on *guanxi*, relationships or personal networks. *Guanxi* also causes corruption and inefficiency and will always prevent China from being a true egalitarian state. Although China is very lucrative for investment, the lack of transparency and information will invariably be a barrier to businesses. Doing business in China is easier because of reforms, but not yet what it should be. The communist party seems to allow—even encourage—Western trends, but it still takes a hard stance toward civil dissent, pursuing it with the same passion as five years ago. Corruption still haunts the country. Peering over the beaches of Zhujiajian are opulent mansions of at least 5,000-10,000 square feet, typically owned by the regional government and used by regional leaders to dine with their *guanxi*. Similarly, opulent mansions equipped with German ultraluxury vehicles for government officials line expensive parts of Beijing. While people in one part of the country become wealthier, people in the other find it extremely difficult or impossible to ameliorate their living conditions. Even those who are on the track to success have their futures determined by the outcome of a tedious exam. Though optimistic, teens recognize the problems of society and feel a sense of "helplessness."

What is befuddling after the West's increased knowledge about China's modernization is the lack of resources diverted to education about China. In addition to not properly preparing youth for survival in the global market, the U.S. education system does not offer Mandarin language courses in its public schools, teaching instead French and Spanish—thereby reaching roughly 550 million speakers combined as opposed to the 1.3 billion Mandarin speakers. As China modernizes further and its Internet usage proliferates, Mandarin will be unquestionably more valuable than French and Spanish; it will eventually overtake English as the most used language on the Internet. Though the excuse of a lack of resources in many schools may be well taken, the French and Spanish language teachers and the school systems' fears of integrating Mandarin into the American curriculum may inhibit American Gen Y from being able to communicate with their counterparts who speak English fluently. Ultimately, it will be the American youth, unprepared for challenges in the global market, who will suffer the most from global competition.

Conclusion: Where Will Gen Y's Path Take Them?

Generation Y is more than a surveyable consortium of consumers; it is the next generation of political and economic leaders of the world. Current assessments of their backgrounds and hopes not only provide the best indicator of this bustling market segment's receptiveness to product, but also show possible points of convergence and possible deviations that could spell trouble in the future.

The ambitious youth live in one of the fastest-growing economies in the world, eclipsing the growth of its neighbors and developed nations. Companies like Ferrari, Bentley, Dior, and Chanel, that would never have thought about penetrating the China market in past years, are now flocking into China to start building the ever-so-important brand name amongst the younger generations. Domestic retail sales are skyrocketing, and the only question is how best to allocate the huge amounts of foreign investment flowing into the Middle Kingdom each day. The government is even planning for a large middle class by building beaches and vacation spots throughout the country. The 2008 Summer Olympics in Beijing and the Shanghai 2010 World Expo will further open up China to the world.

Generation Y looks to the future for prospects of vast national growth as well as individual economic growth promised by their country's acceptance of capitalism. In so doing, China has allowed them to become more Westernized, contradicting the ideology of the past 50 years. It embraces entrepreneurship and has integrated the Internet into its daily lives, becoming part of a larger, connected audience of world events. Should China maintain the status quo, the youth can rightfully expect to increase their income and improve their standard of living. The larger goal for them and their nation is full economic development in the arena of global capitalism. All ends justify the means, and there is no turning back until the goal is accomplished—meaning there will be significant changes and problems for the youth.

The youth's end product is a booming internal consumer economy that will in time rival that of the United States. The world economy will be affected by the prolific number of consumers in this generation. As they mature into middle-aged adults and a healthier economy emerges, Gen Y can expand its nation's economy prior to its retirement as did the baby boomers in the U.S. China, specifically Shanghai, will be a key force in successful overseas transactions, as corporations will feed the imports China needs to produce its exports.

In opening the country, the youth have to acclimate themselves to the outside world, to unheard of ideas, and to foreign peoples. They are now bombarded by foreign influences that tell them what to do without a proper explanation of why. In an age when the Internet is becoming more prevalent and the information sought is more readily available, the Chinese youth will quickly become experts on foreign trade and high-tech products. They will know how to get the products they seek, and foreign companies will know how to get their message to them quickly and conveniently. Inadvertently, this generation will reconcile the incongruence between Chinese tradition and Western consumerist ideology. While fulfilling their filial roles, they will also inundate themselves with material items more so than preceding generations. Moreover, the youth will define and create China's modern culture. Playing with fads and trends right now, the youth will choose that which best suits them, taking with them the more organized aspects of Western culture. However, the youth will not relinquish their cultural heritage, which they view as better and natural. Like the Japanese who modernized in their own fashion, they will create a sinocised (Chinese-influenced) version of Westernization.

China's Generation Y will be the first generation to permanently define China's currently amorphous corporate world, creating the standard in which the business of the future will be conducted. It will bring China's information technology to the vanguard of cutting-edge technology, and further develop the entertainment and financial industries. It will also take China's aerospace industry to farther distances, having already conducted five successful missions into space and put forth a timetable for its own space station to be in orbit within nine years. The youth will not only build their nation into a leading economy, but will also affect world politics as China is further integrated into the world community. China's strategic position in East Asian politics makes it a major force in the United Nations Security Council, where it holds a permanent seat and can veto resolutions from the U.S.; its military buildup has the power to put the whole region and the U.S. on edge.

Though it is easy to refute the indications of China becoming a superpower and an economic giant, one must consider the impressive history of the Chinese. Asian cultures have always held an admirable work ethic. The Japanese are known to work long hours, and the Koreans are known to exact much from their fellow business partners. The Chinese are by no means exempt from this pattern. Depletion of resources, burgeoning population, and corruption made China poor—not the work ethic of its people. China's leaders are gaining authority in micro- and macropolitics, specifically in the Korean peninsula and Taiwan. The Chinese government is decentralizing its power, giving more autonomy to provinces. These provinces are now competing with one another to lure more foreign investment.

206

The youth face many obstacles, chief among them an education system whose values are incongruous with Western capitalistic values; a legal system full of loopholes and unequipped to handle business quarrels; traditional values such as *guanxi* that invariably make business function inefficiently; and overprotective parents who shield obstacles. They also face fixing one of the largest socioeconomic divides between the haves and the have-nots in the world.

Furthermore, the youth are amidst a sea of influences and ideas, following ideals of which they know relatively little. Their parents have not taught them or given them commands on how to deal with globalization, choosing instead not to disturb their children's preparations for school entrance exams. While their education system teaches them time-trusted memorization models, it does not teach the flexible skills that allow them to think about how they should function in the global market and the challenges of the future, in contrast to the government and globalization courses offered in American high school curricula. The government is itself conflicted in regard to its own stance on globalization. It needs to produce science and math geniuses for the development of the nation and is reluctant to divert resources to humanities courses.

In contrast, the Japanese youth were taught after WWII how to gain market share and make money in the market, along with the importance of hard work and efficiency. They followed this program and became the leaders of the Mitsubishis and Toyotas of their economy, making Japan the second-largest economy in the world, with corporations that rival Western conglomerates. Similarly, German youth learned the power of building brands and companies like Daimler-Benz and Deutsche bank. In today's world the Chinese youth are building their country's future without a road map, and do not know why they should be working so diligently or where they are going. Mortgages, bills, debt, and computers have been introduced to a "Less Developed Country" within a period of fifteen years. While these youth are faced with one of the fastest rates of change ever, they do not face the political devastation of war, deprivation, and conscription. The pampered, sheltered youth may not understand what it takes for those towering skyscrapers to line the streets of their crowded cities and why their parents have this newfound wealth. Without a proper road map to prepare for the challenges of the 21st century, the Chinese youth are putting both themselves and the world in a precarious situation.

Within 10-20 years these teenagers will be political and economic leaders; it is undetermined whether they have the mindset and understanding of the decisions currently being made in the world. If everything has been handed to them on a silver platter as only children, they may make decisions based on "me" rather than considering the global implications of their decisions. Without concrete long-term goals other than making money, it is difficult to forecast the road the Chinese youth will take—specifically, whether China's 1.3 billion capitalists will work together with the world or spark economic warfare with it. The youth will work hard toward some goal, harder than the West will, but that course has yet to be uncovered. Youth-exchange programs overseas will help open the youth up to the wider picture; communication with peers and knowledge learned on the Internet will also help mitigate this shortcoming.

It is also arguable that with the spoiling and increased wealth stemming from the one-child policy, Generation Y will become indolent, leading China down the wrong path. True, teenagers yearn for the benefits and luxuries of the modern life; and true, some of their energy appears to be low, resembling their American and European counterparts. Though some of China's Gen Y is currently lazy, a very large contingent of them is not: most females in the study, for example, are assiduously working to achieve their own success, most often the gratification of earning money. The zest for success and catching up with the West, the difficultly of making money in China's competitive job market, and the work ethic instilled into them by their parents will be their profound motivations for success.

Their strengths not as individuals but in large numbers give them power. Their education, optimism, ambition to succeed, pragmatism, and motivating obligation to provide for their family contrast with the complacent attitudes of Gen Y in the developed world. What makes the youth stand out more than their grandparents? The enhanced opportunities from globalization have created a near unanimous optimism for entry into the global community. Rather than push such opportunities away, the youth have embraced them.

China's youth are also facing other changes in society. China's intense modernization has produced a chasm between generations greater than any that has existed in the U.S. This large generation gap has a palpable influence on Gen Y's development, and will become more concrete as Western trends and products continue to be favored over Chinese. Critics may believe that generation gaps are inherent in many cultures as a result of rapidly changing subcultures; however, the situation in China is different from, or at least more poignant than, the situation in the United States. Although teenagers might bitterly disagree, American parents are closer in temperament to their children because they grew up during the days of Disney, Elvis, and flower power. They are more liberal in disciplining teenagers because they view teenage experimentation as a part of human development. Polls state that the Generation Y of America is actually closer and can relate more to their baby-boomer parents than its preceding generation, Generation X.

Chinese parents, in contrast, grew up in a "real" communist country, devoid of nearly all that American parents relished in their childhoods. In those years the stereotype of the starving Chinese workers toiling to cultivate rice patties was more or less correct. Chinese parents were governed by an iron hand, both by their government and their parents—certainly not by the personalities of Mickey Mouse and the Rolling Stones. Their horror stories make the "tough childhood" stories of American parents seem benign. The Cultural Revolution changed the careers and potentials of its subjects by "reeducating" scholars and artists, ultimately forcing a great number of the population to "embroider the earth" (work in the fields) in remote provinces. Because the youth have difficulty talking with their parents, some avoid them and consequently have few people with whom to communicate. As a result, some teenagers are unable to deal with emotional shocks and may have trouble enduring future hardship if times get rough for their parents and themselves.

Movies, music, and advertisements now inadvertently extol expression and creativity. Popular soap operas show the more intricate relationships and even divorce, contrasted to a simple, loving, but economically sufficient relationship between male and female. Pirated DVDs of Western movies also depict deficient relationships and divorces to the youth. The youth must struggle with their parents' ideals and those of the West. Marketers facilitate the youth's desires for the accoutrements of a Western life. China's Generation Y now feels the need to have more freedom and leisurely lives that many of the Westernized youth have. They want cell phones, televisions, technological gadgets, and fancy cars, just to name a few.

But although China's Gen Y is seen as a generation on the verge of a cultural rebellion, the extent of such rebellion may be overstated. The Chinese students live in a society which encourages completely dissimilar qualities from American society. China encourages students never to question authority of parents, school, and government. Parents and society already determine the lives of their offspring. Society is unique in that everybody is accepted and fits in like clockwork. Chinese teenagers generally accept this but are more likely than previous generations to rebel against it. Oddly enough, teenagers who acknowledged their acceptance of the new culture and who have expressed discontent at their parents' intrusiveness have also stated that they will not be the ones to change the Chinese family. Generation Y will not be the one group to abandon thousands of years of tradition for any new trend, though Gen Yers yearn for both individualism and freedom. But these changes and influences have indeed made their mark on them, and Generation Y is more confused than ever.

Kenichi Ohmae, a management guru and political adviser, contends that youth entrenched in gaming and technology, such as in China and Japan, have for the first time in history a significant commonality between them—computers—and in the future generations such as China's Generation Y will create a new civilization similar to the way new ideas caused the breakup of European society in earlier centuries. According to historian Oscar Handling, the institutions that bound people disappeared through a "brutal filter" created by disenfranchised people who were victimized by those institutions. Ohmae believes that the global economy is rapidly expanding and creating new ideas for young generations around the world. Eventually these ideas will lead to societies that do not obsess over class systems and stringent social norms. These "Nintendo generations" are pledging allegiance to the global economy, eventually leading to the nation-state's end. This position on Generation Y is to be expected, since Gen Yers have a higher propensity than previous generations to remain indoors to play games in a virtual reality. Adults are beginning to fear the influence of technology and information on children, and especially of their wider interest in a more global society. Americans are not exempt from this fear, because they reelected George W. Bush to preserve the traditional conservative values of their society. The administration has attempted to censor what society deems inappropriate for youth on television and the Internet. Religious groups that historically have been supportive of conservative governments have blamed immigration, the perceived collapse of family life, homosexuality, and feminism as the corruptive influences on today's youth. Like the Chinese government, the American government has

211

attempted to limit accessibility of "corruptive material" viewed by children, albeit in a less obvious manner.

China's Generation Y is united with other foreign Gen Y's by the influences that the founders of the Peoples' Republic felt would destroy them. They love Western-style music and fashion that starkly differ from the xenophobic sentiments of the preceding generation. Via the Internet teenagers in China can connect with teenagers in India and America, France and South Africa, and can accept advice from strangers who have also distanced themselves from their parents. It would seem that life is no longer about the continuity of a government built on the values of the community, but of the pursuit of individual happiness.

China's Generation Y can appear at first glance to be a threat to China's sovereignty. It does not owe allegiance to government officials in Beijing; it owes allegiance to technology, consumerism, pleasure, and to a lesser extent, freedom and cosmopolitanism. It lives by the devices and ideas that the government heavily monitors and regulates. The amount of time the central government can sustain the world's largest economic disparity is limited. However, it is important to remember that Generation Y strongly adheres to traditional ideals of family and friendship. Although Kenichi Ohmae is on target with an isolated youth, the dissolution of the nation-state will not occur in Generation Y's lifetime.

American companies should market to this generation because it will become a major market. As seen through KFC's business strategy in China and the success of famous Chinese pop singers, U.S. companies need to create advertising campaigns aimed at the youth that emphasize the freedom and pride of being a youth. Firms must also emphasize luxury, beauty, and coolness to the youth, for a Ferrari is surely more appetizing than a Chevrolet. To gain a wider market with a larger purchasing power, they need to market products to parents and grandparents, paying close attention to cultural and societal norms. For instance, marketing a brand of vitamins to increase the stamina of students before entrance exams could strike a nerve in parents who will buy anything for the success of their little emperor. Moreover, following the youth's reasoning, raising the price on a pleasing product guarantees that it is of high quality. And if convinced the product is of high quality, teens are prone to buy it, believing that it will last longer. China's entrance into the WTO and increased efforts at improving the business environment will reduce some of the problems of doing business there. However, many foreign companies go bust in China because they do not conduct adequate market research and do not have the contacts necessary for doing business. The youth's lifestyles, disposable incomes, preferences, and needs specific to each market all must be figured into a strategic business plan before companies court them.

We can be confident in believing that in the future we will see today's Chinese teenagers sitting across from us at the negotiating table, be it business or politics. We have yet to discover whether in the future the awakened dragon will be as docile as it is now, but we should enhance the bonds between our two cultures and learn how to ensure that we remain symbiotic friends, not virulent enemies. I trust that with this book we can further the understanding of the Chinese youth and lay the foundations for a cooperative relationship between the East and the West.

Generation Y has a voice, though it is now faint, and our choice of whether or not to listen to it will determine the future of the American economy, the Chinese economy, and the ever-increasing importance of the global economy. Thus I leave you with a statement, a cliff-hanger of some sort, one which China's Gen Y would want to relay to America:

"Everyone will speak fluent English, and we will be a developed country rather than a developing country. We will be better than America."

CHINESE-U.S. CURRENCY EXCHANGE RATES
1982-2005

(Based on Chinese RMB per U.S. Dollar, RMB/US$)

Year	Rate
1982	1.92
1983	1.98
1984	2.79
1985	3.20
1986	3.71
1987	3.72
1988	3.72
1989	4.72
1990	5.23
1991	5.40
1992	5.84
1993	5.81
1994	8.44
1995	8.32
1996	8.33
1997	8.31
1998	8.28
1999	8.28
2000	8.28
2001	8.28
2002	8.28
2003	8.28
2004	8.28
2005	8.11

Sources: Datastream and CIA China fact sheets

BIBLIOGRAPHY

Backman, Michael. *Big in Asia: 25 Strategies for Business Success*. New York: Palgrave Macmillan, 2003.

Belden, Elionne L. W. *Claiming Chinese Identity*. New York: Garland Publishing, 1997.

"China Begins Massive Census." (2000). BBC News Online. Retrieved May 15, 2004, from http://news.bbc.co.uk/1/hi/world/asia-pacific/1000357.stm.

"China Steps Up One-Child Policy." (2000). BBC News Online. Retrieved May 15, 2004, from http://news.bbc.co.uk/1/hi/world/asia-pacific/941511.stm.

Choi, Ching & Penny Kane. (1999). "China's One-Child Family Policy." Retrieved May 15, 2004, from Website: http://bmj.bmjjournals.com/cgi/content/full/319/7215/992.

Evans, Karin. *The Lost Daughters of China: Abandoned Girls, Their Journey to America and the Search for a Missing Past*. New York : J.P. Tarcher/Putnam, 2000.

Faber, Marc. (2004). "Should You Buy What China Buys?" Retrieved May 15, 2004, from http://www.ameinfo.com/news/Detailed/37659.html.

Faison, Seth. (1997). "Chinese Are Happily Breaking the One-Child Rule." Retrieved May 15, 2004, from Website: http://www.mtholyoke.edu/acad/intrel/chinpop.htm.

Fewsmith, Joseph. *China since Tiananmen: The Politics of Transition*. New York: Cambridge University Press, 2001.

Godfrey, Mark. "Pretty Profitable." Retrieved May 15, 2004, from Website: http://www.chinatoday.com.cn/English/e2004/e200404/p18.htm.

Gottschang, Suzanne, and Lyn Jeffery. *China Urban*. Durham, NC: Duke University Press, 2001.

Jing, Jun. *Feeding China's Little Emperors*. Stanford: Stanford University Press, 2000.

Lynch, David J. "China Finds Western Ways Bring New Woes." *USA Today,* May 19, 2004, 13A, 14A.

Matuszak, Sascha. (2001). "An American in China." Retrieved May 15, 2004, from Website: http://www.antiwar.com/matuszak/ma061901.html.

Nichols, Bill & Peronet Despeignes. (2003). "Taiwan, Trade Test Strength of U.S.-China Ties." Retrieved May 15, 2004, from *USA Today* Website: http://www.jsonline.com/bym/News/aug03/162995.asp.

Peterson, Glen. *Education, Culture, and Identity in Twentieth-Century China.* Ann Arbor: University of Michigan Press, 2001.

Schifferes, Steve. (2000). "The UN and World Poverty." Retrieved May 15, 2004, from BBC News Website: http://news.bbc.co.uk/1/hi/business/906238.stm.

Schmid, John. (2003). "Chinese Yuan Irks U.S. Business: Fixed Exchange Rate Gives Beijing An Advantage." Retrieved May 15, 2004, from *Journal Sentinel* Website: http://www.jsonline.com/bym/News/aug03/162995.asp.

Simpson, Ian. (2000). "China's Youth: Shaping the Future. " Retrieved May 15, 2004, from BBC News Website: http://news.bbc.co.uk/1/hi/world/asia-pacific/1001366.stm.

Starr, John Bryan. *Understanding China: A Guide to China's Economy, History, and Political Structure.* New York: Hill & Wang, 1997.

Tung, May Pao-may. *Chinese Americans and Their Immigrant Parents: Conflict, Identity, and Values.* New York: Haworth Clinical Practice Press, 2000.

Whitcomb, Vanessa Lide. *The Complete Idiot's Guide to Modern China.* Indianapolis: Alpha Books, 2003.

Woronov, Naomi. *China through My Window.* Armonk, N.Y.: M.E. Sharpe, 1988.

Zhang, Jialin. "U.S.-China Trade Issues after the WTO and the PNTR Deal: A Chinese Perspective." Retrieved May 15, 2004, from Website: http://www-hoover.stanford.edu/publications/epp/103/103b.html.

INDEX

All-China Youth Federation, 28
America, 2, 21, 30, 51, 80, 83, 89,
    108, 123, 133, 135-36, 142,
    144-46, 149-50, 179, 212, 213
American, 1-3, 19, 31, 35, 46, 55,
    60, 73, 90, 95, 102, 105, 112,
    121, 124, 133, 151-52, 173-76,
    200-1, 211
American curriculum (school),
    34-35, 45, 204, 207
American foreign policy, 148-50
American Generation Y, x, xv-
    xvi, 6, 8-9, 16, 19-21, 26, 31,
    33-35, 41, 50, 52, 56, 59, 76,
    80, 96-97, 143, 170, 172, 181,
    200, 204, 208-9
American parents, xv, 15, 28, 46,
    96, 187, 200, 209, 210
Anti-Secession law, 146
ASEAN (Association of
    Southeast Asian Nations),
    149-50, 155
Asia Cup, 71. *See also* Asian
    Soccer Cup
Asian Soccer Cup, 147
Auto insurance, 117
Basketball Without Borders,
    157
Being different, 82
Beijing, ix-x, 16-18, 25-26, 28-30,
    37, 51-52, 58, 61, 66, 73, 76-
    77, 81, 83, 92, 94, 108, 116-18,
    123, 141, 146, 148, 159-60,
    163, 170, 173, 178-79, 201-4,
    212, 218n

Buckalew, Lauren, 38, 91, 161
Bush administration, 55, 149
Business, ix, x, xvi, 10, 14, 16, 43,
    51, 77, 102-3, 112, 129, 136,
    159-60, 162, 169, 195, 202-3,
    206-7, 212-13
BusinessWeek, 3
Capitalism, 16, 23, 47, 96, 138,
    159, 196, 204-5
Carrefour, 115, 144, 184, 190, 192
CBC Market Research, xvi, 9,
    38, 91, 137
CCTV, 74, 134
Channel Young, 57, 74
Chen Tao, 141
China Central Television. *See*
    CCTV
China Youth and Children
    Research Center, 29
Chinese government, xvii, 5, 24-
    25, 55, 78, 80, 120, 124, 137-
    38, 146-49, 152, 159, 206, 211
Chinese school system, 39, 42,
    70. *See also* Education
    system
Chinese teaching methods, 39
College entrance exam, 37-38, 88
Communism, xi, 14, 22-24, 28, 47,
    149, 159
Communist Party of China
    (CPC), 24, 27, 103, 145, 203
Confucian (tradition, idea,
    doctrine, teaching, thought),
    24, 38, 87, 90, 100, 102, 104n,
    106, 169, 198, 201

Confucianism, 102

Confucius, 87

Consumerism, xii, xvii, 2, 4, 15-16, 18, 75, 95-96, 155, 176, 184, 193, 196, 212

Consumerist values, 23

Consumption, 102, 111, 122, 165

COSPLAY, 58, 141

Cousins, 31, 91

Covey, Stephen, 78

Cui Jian, 52-53

Cultural Revolution (1966-76), xi, 2, 26, 97, 122, 161, 172, 210

Dating, 33, 46-47, 92-93, 98, 130, 173

Decentralization, 159

Deforestation, 142-43

Deng Xiaoping, 27, 75

Dependent, 6, 31, 88-90, 95, 199

Divorce, 90, 98-99, 130, 210

Divorce Chinese Style, 99

Education system, 5, 15, 20, 26, 34, 41, 44, 133, 143, 199, 202-3, 207. *See also* Chinese school system

Elton, Chester, 77-78

Entrepreneurship, 78, 129, 137, 140, 205

Evictions/land grabs, 109

Family structure, 171

Fast food, 55, 109, 111-12, 114, 173, 177, 183, 188, 190-91, 193

Fears, 19, 65-66, 91, 204

Federalism, 133

Filial piety, 87-88, 94, 100, 106, 131

Foreign investment, 6-7, 18, 137, 156, 204, 206

Foreign joint ventures, 136

Formula One, 73

Fuxing High School, 46

General Administration for Industry and Commerce, 65

Generation gap, 15, 32, 42, 93-94, 96-97, 196, 209

Globalization, 124, 207, 209

Goss, Peter, 150

Governmental corruption, 26

Grandparents, 53, 62, 89-90, 93, 98, 106, 114, 155, 171, 174, 195, 209, 212

Guangdong (province), 53, 160

Guanxi, 90, 102-3, 138, 203, 207

Handling, Oscar, 211

Healthcare, 122, 124, 144, 157, 164, 191-92

Heinz, 178

Hong Kong, 17-18, 51, 53, 55, 76, 99, 108, 115, 132, 136, 159-60, 163-64, 178

Housing arrangements, 106

Hutong, 108

Individual investment, 137

Individual roles, 87

Inheritance, 91, 171

InterMedia, 63-64

Internal consumer economy, 205

Internet Café, 17, 25, 59, 66, 70, 98

Internet friendships, 70

Internet users, 25, 60, 63, 67

James, Lebron, 176

Jiangsu (province), 114

Jordan, Michael, 71

Karaoke, 21, 35, 50-51, 115
Kentucky Fried Chickens. *See* KFC
KFC, 20, 72, 111, 114, 141, 158-59, 177, 188, 191-92, 197-98
KFC Championships, 72
Koizumi, Junichiro, 147
"Little emperor," 31, 90, 170, 200, 213
Maglev (train), 44
Mao Zedong, 27, 29, 50, 75, 77, 82, 114, 172
Marriage, 6, 90, 130
McDonald's, 63, 83, 111, 114, 129, 137, 141, 158, 178, 188, 192, 197-98
Memorization, 24, 39, 90, 207
Meng Sun, 141
Merkle, Charles, xiii, 137
Mingong (rural workers), 144
Ministry of Education, 40
Mobile phone market, 25, 79
Modernization, xvii, 4, 16-17, 27, 40, 77, 92-93, 95-96, 105, 110, 118, 122, 124, 140, 171, 184-85, 203, 209
MTV, 50, 53, 56, 74
Nanjing Road (Shanghai), 83, 175, 182, 201
NBA, 71-72, 121, 157, 178
New York Times, The, 85, 150
Nike, 72, 176, 179-82, 191-92, 199
North Korea, 149
Obesity, 114
Ohmae, Kenichi, 211-12
Oil, 6, 119, 148, 165
Olympic Games, 17, 73, 179, 204

One-Child Policy, 29-31, 90-91, 111, 161, 172, 208
Oriental Department Store, 181
Oriental Oasis, 72
Peer pressure, 34-35, 50
Penalties, 30
Piracy, 54, 123, 202
Pizza Hut, 158, 192
Pollution, 106, 117-19, 143
Population, xi, xvii, 1-3, 5, 7-8, 16, 29-30, 41, 56, 60, 114, 121, 124, 136-37, 144, 155-57, 161, 163, 165, 200, 206, 210
Population peak, 155, 166n
Porter, Michael, 78
Propaganda, 145-46, 148, 150
Pudong Area (Shanghai), xv, 44
Purchasing power, 4, 8, 36, 80, 111, 115, 155, 169, 170, 173-74, 180-82, 195
Rape of Nanjing, 147
Rebellion, 4, 15, 97-98, 144, 210
Red envelope, 174
Retail sales, 180, 204
Revenue surplus, 2
Rural, 15, 27, 30, 35, 37, 59, 80, 94, 103, 106, 108-9, 111, 121, 136-37, 144, 160, 162-65, 172-73, 180, 193
Sanlitun area (Beijing), 83
Shanghai, xiii, xv, xvi, 9, 11-12, 14, 16-18, 21, 30, 37-38, 40, 44, 46, 50-51, 61, 71-73, 75-76, 79, 83, 91, 93, 99, 101, 103, 106-9, 111, 114-16, 118, 120-21, 123-24, 132, 136-38, 140-41, 147, 159-60, 163, 173, 175, 178, 181-82, 184, 197-201, 204-5

Shanghai Stock Exchange, 137
Shenzhen, 164, 173
Sichuan, 41, 141, 160
SIS International Research (New York), xiii
Socioeconomic gap, 138, 143
Special Economic Zones, 163
Spitting, 108, 140
Starbucks, 158, 191
State-owned companies, 90, 140, 143
Stress, 41-43, 50-51, 60, 92, 99
Sun Nan, 54
Taiwan, 5, 51, 54-55, 76, 80, 132, 138, 140, 143, 145-47, 150-51, 163, 206
Television, 2, 6, 28, 43, 50, 53, 55-56, 59, 64, 67, 69, 73-77, 111, 115, 132, 158, 174-76, 178, 184, 211
Television during the 1980s, 75
Test performance, 91
Tiananmen Square, 5, 25, 146
Traditional Chinese culture, 49, 94, 125. *See also* Traditional culture
Traditional culture, 20, 26, 99, 124. *See also* Traditional Chinese culture
Tse, Nicholas, 51
Tuition, 27, 36
Unemployment, 4, 131, 138, 143, 160-61
United Nations, 5, 8, 138, 155, 206
United Nations Security Council, 5, 206

United States of America. *See* America
University, xii, 5, 10-11, 24, 26, 37-38, 41-43, 46, 65-66, 78-79, 88, 91, 115, 128, 130-131, 135-141, 148, 157, 175-76, 178, 199
Urban, xvi, 3-4, 15-16, 21, 27, 29, 36, 49, 51, 58, 66, 76, 79-80, 82-83, 94, 106, 108, 111, 114-15, 117, 120, 124, 144, 162-65, 170, 179-80, 199
Wal-Mart, 2, 137, 164, 192
Wan Baoqi, 30
Wang Shan, 141
Wang ZhiZhi, 72
Washington Post, The, 30-31
Welfare, 15, 26, 133, 136, 144, 157
Western evils, xvi, xvii, 26
World Trade Organization (WTO), xi, 3, 55, 117, 140, 155, 159-60, 213
Xiao huangdi. See "Little emperor"
Xinhua Bookstore network, 78
Xujiahui Road (Shanghai), 182
Yao Ming, 71-72, 158, 178
Yu Haiting, 65
Zhangjiagang, 143
Zhejiang (province), 123
Zheng Qingming, 40
Zhengs, the (Shanghai home stay), xiii, 134, 197-201
Zhou, Jay, 51, 186
Zhujiajian, 123, 203

◪ Homa & Sekey Books Titles on China

The Haier Way:
The Making of a Chinese Business Leader and a Global Brand
By Jeannie J. Yi, Ph.D., & Shawn X. Ye, MBA
ISBN: 1-931907-01-3, Hardcover, Business, $24.95

Haier is the largest consumer appliance maker in China. The book traces the appliance giant's path to success, from its early bleak years to becoming the world's 5th largest household appliance manufacturer. The book explains how Haier excelled in quality, service, technology innovation, a global vision and a management style that is a blend of Jack Welch of "GE" and Confucius of ancient China.

"I enjoyed reading through it – A great story! Haier is certainly an impressive company."
— **Jack Welch**, former GE Chairman and CEO

"The book throws light on a number of important issues about China's development path...comprehensive and up-to-date...highly readable."
— **Dr. N.T. Wang,** Director of China-International Business Project, Columbia University

Foreign managers will find that the book's greatest strength is that it reveals successful techniques for managing and integrating formerly state-owned enterprises into entrepreneurial companies in China .... As the first to recognize the significance of the Haier story, Yi and Ye deserve praise for bringing to light the first of what will eventually be many Chinese company success stories.
— **The China Business Review**, January-February 2004

Haier is one of the few Chinese companies with a real chance to become a global player in the near future, yet ironically most of us have no idea what it means to be inside a Chinese enterprise. This book takes us inside of Haier so that we understand just what makes Haier work so well and what it is that differentiates Haier from the others."
— **Professor William A. Fischer,** International Institute for Management Development

Homa & Sekey Books Titles on China

China's Generation Y:
Understanding the Future Leaders of the World's Next Superpower
By Michael Stanat, United Nations International School
Order No 1029, ISBN 1931907250, Hardcover, 6 x 9, 222 pp., $24.95
Order No 1040, ISBN 1931907323, Paperback, 6 x 9, 222 pp., $17.95
Contemporary Affairs, 2006

Based upon interviews and surveys conducted in Shanghai by the author, this is the first English book to look into all aspects of China's young generation — their life styles, relationships with family and society, views, dreams and development... Growing up during the information age, China's Generation Y (born between 1981 and 1995) will most likely be the political and business leaders of the world's next superpower by the year 2025. *China's Generation Y* provides an exciting look into the lives and minds of China's youth, showing Western readers who they are, how they got there, and where they are headed. The book brings to life the influences on them – political, cultural, family, economic, and environmental – in such a way that it truly provides a rare glimpse into the minds of today's youth and tomorrow's leaders.

Stanat's work is a laudable contribution, as it provides a comprehensive study on China's Generation Y, ranging from its socio-political consequences to the generational gap and the economic factors that ensue. This research builds a more nuanced and objective understanding of this generation.
— **Eva H. Shi,** former editor-in-chief, *Harvard Asia Pacific Review*

As someone who lived and worked in China for several years [as a management consultant with McKinsey & Company in Beijing], I was struck by how closely Michael Stanat's accounts resonated with my own observations and experiences.
— **Christopher J. Fry,** president, Strategic Management Solutions Group

⑤ Homa & Sekey Books Titles on China

Willow Leaf, Maple Leaf: A Novel of Immigration Blues
By David Ke, PhD
Order No 1036, ISBN: 1931907242
5 ½ x 8 ½, Paperback, 2006, 203 pp., $16.95
Fiction/Asian-American Studies

Willow Leaf, Maple Leaf . . . is a novel that weaves fantasy and cultural myth into a story about immigration, moral and sexual dilemmas, and cultural and gender barriers. Willow Leaf is a dazzlingly beautiful Chinese woman who is smuggled to Canada. While working at a sweatshop and at a massage parlor—and through several extramarital affairs—she learns that survival in a different country might mean a compromise of morals. When her husband visits her, she realizes that he is not as she remembers him. He, in turn, refuses the money she offers him and her request for him to move their family to Canada, and returns to China alone. Eventually, she finds new wealth and new love with an elderly man and has her own successful business. But can Willow Leaf truly leave her love for her family and China behind?

Paintings by Xu Jin:
Tradition and Innovation in Chinese Fine Brushwork
By Xu Jin, preface by Prof. Robert E. Harrist, Jr., Columbia University
Order No 1028, ISBN 1931907234, Hardcover, 10 ½ x 10 ½, 128 pp.,
color illustrations throughout, $39.50
Art

This book brings together over seventy Chinese fine brushwork paintings by Xu Jin, including figures, landscapes, animals, flowers and birds. Drawing on sources in earlier art and traditional iconography, Xu Jin's paintings are characterized by stylish composition, impressive colors, and fine lines. They not only demonstrate a natural integration of verse, calligraphy, painting and seal, but also a fine combination of Chinese and Western painting skills.

⚘ Homa & Sekey Books Titles on China

Flower Terror: Suffocating Stories of China by Pu Ning
ISBN 0-9665421-0-X, Fiction, Paperback, $13.95

"The stories in this work are well written." – Library Journal

Acclaimed Chinese writer eloquently describes the oppression of intellectuals in his country between 1950s and 1970s in these twelve autobiographical novellas and short stories. Many of the stories are so shocking and heart-wrenching that one cannot but feel suffocated.

The Peony Pavilion: A Novel by Xiaoping Yen, Ph.D.
ISBN 0-9665421-2-6, Fiction, Paperback, $16.95

"A window into the Chinese literary imagination." – Publishers Weekly

A sixteen-year-old girl visits a forbidden garden and falls in love with a young man she meets in a dream. She has an affair with her dream-lover and dies longing for him. After her death, her unflagging spirit continues to wait for her dream-lover. Does her lover really exist? Can a youthful love born of a garden dream ever blossom? The novel is based on a sixteenth-century Chinese opera written by Tang Xianzu, "the Shakespeare of China."

Butterfly Lovers: A Tale of the Chinese Romeo and Juliet
By Fan Dai, Ph.D., ISBN 0-9665421-4-2, Fiction, Paperback, $16.95

"An engaging, compelling, deeply moving, highly recommended and rewarding novel." – Midwest Books Review

A beautiful girl disguises herself as a man and lives under one roof with a young male scholar for three years without revealing her true identity. They become sworn brothers, soul mates and lovers. In a world in which marriage is determined by social status and arranged by parents, what is their inescapable fate?

⬛ Homa & Sekey Books Titles on China

The Dream of the Red Chamber: An Allegory of Love
By Jeannie Jinsheng Yi, Ph.D., ISBN: 0-9665421-7-7, Hardcover
Asian Studies/Literary Criticism, $49.95

Although dreams have been studied in great depth about this most influential classic Chinese fiction, the study of all the dreams as a sequence and in relation to their structural functions in the allegory is undertaken here for the first time.

Always Bright: Paintings by American Chinese Artists 1970-1999
Edited by Xue Jian Xin et al.
ISBN 0-9665421-3-4, Art, Hardcover, $49.95

"An important, groundbreaking, seminal work." – Midwest Book Review

A selection of paintings by eighty acclaimed American Chinese artists in the late 20th century, *Always Bright* is the first of its kind in English publication. The album falls into three categories: oil painting, Chinese painting and other media painting. It also offers profiles of the artists and information on their professional accomplishment.

Always Bright, Vol. II: Paintings by Chinese American Artists
Edited by Eugene Wang, Harvard Univ., et al.
ISBN: 0-9665421-6-9, Art, Hardcover, $50.00

A sequel to the above, the book includes artworks of ninety-two artists in oil painting, Chinese painting, watercolor painting, and other media such as mixed media, acrylic, pastel, pen and pencil, etc. The book also provides information on the artists and their professional accomplishment. Artists included come from different backgrounds, use different media and belong to different schools. Some of them enjoy international fame while others are enterprising young men and women who are more impressionable to novelty and singularity.

Homa & Sekey Books Titles on China

Ink Paintings by Gao Xingjian, the Nobel Prize Winner
ISBN: 1-931907-03-X, Hardcover, Art, $34.95

An extraordinary art book by the Nobel Prize Winner for Literature in 2000, this volume brings together over sixty ink paintings by Gao Xingjian that are characteristic of his philosophy and painting style. Gao believes that the world cannot be explained, and the images in his paintings reveal the black-and-white inner world that underlies the complexity of human existence. People admire his meditative images and evocative atmosphere by which Gao intends his viewers to visualize the human conditions in extremity.

Splendor of Tibet: The Potala Palace, Jewel of the Himalayas
By Phuntsok Namgyal
ISBN: 1-931907-02-1, Hardcover, Art/Architecture, $39.95

A magnificent and spectacular photographic book about the Potala Palace, the palace of the Dalai Lamas and the world's highest and largest castle palace. Over 150 rare and extraordinary color photographs of the Potala Palace are showcased in the book, including murals, thang-ka paintings, stupa-tombs of the Dalai Lamas, Buddhist statues and scriptures, porcelain vessels, enamel work, jade ware, brocade, Dalai Lamas' seals, and palace exteriors.

Musical Qigong:
Ancient Chinese Healing Art from a Modern Master
By Shen Wu, ISBN: 0-9665421-5-0, Health, Paperback, $14.95

Musical Qigong is a special healing energy therapy that combines two ancient Chinese traditions-healing music and Qigong. This guide contains two complete sets of exercises with photo illustrations and discusses how musical Qigong is related to the five elements in the ancient Chinese concept of the universe - metal, wood, water, fire, and earth.

⑤ Homa & Sekey Books Titles on China

Breaking Grounds:
The Journal of a Top Chinese Woman Manager in Retail
by Bingxin Hu, translated from the Chinese by Chengchi Wang, Prefaced
by Professor Louis B. Barnes of Harvard Business School
ISBN: 1-931907-15-3, 256 pp, Hardcover, Business, $24.95

The book records the experience of a Chinese business woman who pioneered and succeeded in modernizing the aging Chinese retail business. Based on her years of business experience, the author recounts the turmoil, clashes of concepts and behind-the-scene decisions in the Chinese retail business, as well as psychological shocks, emotional perplexes, and intellectual apprehension she had gone through.

www.homabooks.com

ORDERING INFORMATION: U.S.: $5.00 for the first item, $1.50 for each additional item. **Outside U.S.**: $10.00 for the first item, $5.00 for each additional item. All major credit cards accepted. You may also send a check or money order in U.S. fund (payable to Homa & Sekey Books) to: Orders Department, Homa & Sekey Books, P. O. Box 103, Dumont, NJ 07628 U.S.A. Tel: 800-870-HOMA; 201-261-8810. Fax: 201-384-6055; 201-261-8890. Email: info@homabooks.com